games 2

THE ideas LIBRARY

FOR YOUTH GROUPS

Youth Specialties

ZondervanPublishingHouse
Grand Rapids, Michigan
A Division of HarperCollinsPublishers

Project editor: Vicki Newby
Cover and interior design: Curt Sell
Art director: Mark Rayburn

ISBN 0-310-22031-9

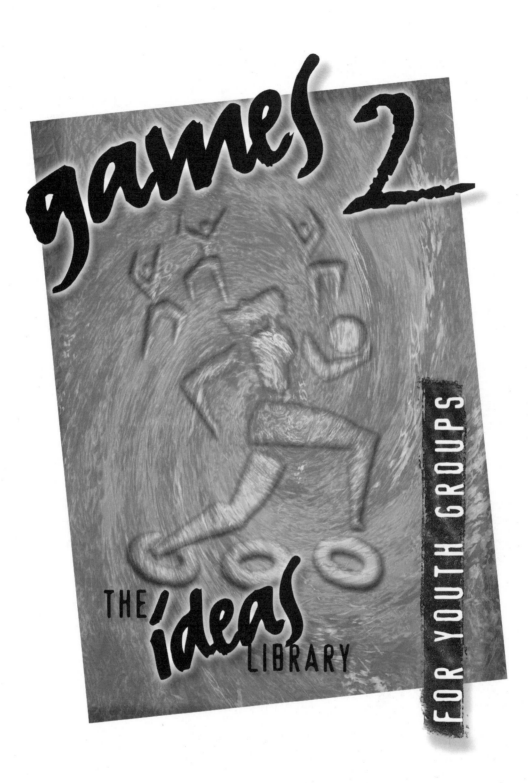

games 2

THE ideas LIBRARY

FOR YOUTH GROUPS

THE IDEAS LIBRARY

Administration, Publicity, & Fundraising
Camps, Retreats, Missions, & Service Ideas
Creative Meetings, Bible Lessons, & Worship Ideas
Crowd Breakers & Mixers
Discussion & Lesson Starters
Discussion & Lesson Starters 2
Drama, Skits, & Sketches
Games
Games 2
Holiday Ideas
Special Events

CONTENTS

6

7

So what killer game have you invented lately?

Are your kids still talking about that game you invented for last month's party? Youth Specialties pays $25 (and in some cases, more) for unpublished, field-tested ideas that have worked for you.

You've probably been in youth work long enough to realize that sanitary, theoretical, tidy ideas aren't what in-the-trenches youth workers are looking for. They want—*you* want—imagination and take-'em-by-surprise novelty in parties and other events. Ideas that have been tested and tempered and improved in the very real, very adolescent world you work in.

So here's what to do:
• Sit down at your computer, get your killer game out of your head and onto your hard drive, then e-mail it to ideas@youthspecialties.com. Or print it off and fax it to 619-440-4939 (Attn: Ideas).
• If you need to include diagrams, photos, art, or samples that help explain your game, stick it all in an envelope and mail it to our street address: Ideas, 1224 Greenfield Dr., El Cajon, CA 92021-3399.
• Be sure to include your name and all your addresses and numbers.
• Let us have about three months to give your game idea a thumbs up or down*, and a little longer for your 25 bucks.

*Hey, no offense intended if your idea isn't accepted. It's just that our fussy Ideas Library editor has these *really* meticulous standards. If the game isn't creative, original, and just plain fun in an utterly wild or delightful way, she'll reject it (reluctantly, though, because she has a tender heart). Sorry. But we figure you deserve only the best game ideas.

Baseball and Kickball Games

The national pastime is hereby turned on its ear by more nutty variations than you can shake a Louisville Slugger at. Most of these games are designed so that anyone can play, regardless of athletic ability. In addition to offshoots of baseball, you'll find here variations of other diamond games, like kickball.

BASEBALL WITH STRINGS ATTACHED

Here's a variation of softball that allows a mixed group to have a competitive softball game. With a regular softball some people have a hard time hitting the ball out of the infield and thus are branded "easy outs." So instead of using a softball and bat, use a tennis ball and tennis racquet. Anyone can hit a good shot, and it's almost impossible to strike out. (If some guys hit it too far with the new equipment, make them use a racquetball racquet or a regular bat.) This game is especially good for larger groups—with 15 or more people on a side. *Marshall Shelley*

BAT-ROUND RELAY

Divide your group into teams. Each team gets a baseball bat that is placed on one end of the playing area, with the team lined up at the other end. The object of this relay is for each team member to run to the bat, put his or her forehead on the bat (in a vertical position), and run around the bat 10 times while in that position. The player then returns to the team, usually so dizzy that getting back to the team is a difficult, but fun to watch, experience. *David Parke*

BLIND ONE-LEGGED KICKBALL

When other baseball-diamond games get old, try this variation: All fielders can move about only on one leg, flamingo style, and must throw with their "odd" arm (right-handers, for example, must throw with only their left arms). Furthermore, all kickers are blindfolded; coaches stationed at each base yell out directions to their runners.

It's as hilarious to watch as to play—and it can easily become a discussion starter as well (our dependence on each other, trust, etc.). *Paul Bertelson*

CRAZY BASEBALL

Create teams of five or more players. With a Nerf ball and bat, play like regular baseball. Here's the crazy part: After a hit, batters can run to any base—

but they cannot run through the pitcher's circle. Base runners score not by touching home plate, but by touching all three bases—first, second, and third—though in any order. Teams get six outs.

David Killinger and Chris Moore

CUP IT

Here is a field game that can be played indoors in a large room without carpeting. Break the group into two equal teams. Team A is at bat first and sits behind home plate. Team B is in the field and is scattered about the room.

A player from Team A throws a Ping-Pong ball from home plate into the field from no lower than shoulder height. Team B players catch the ball with a paper cup in as few bounces as possible. Team A receives a point for each time the ball bounces on the floor before being cupped. (Set a maximum at 15, due to the dribble effect of the ball just before it rolls.) Use a couple of referees to keep track of the bounces. Each member of the team gets one throw, and then the other team comes to bat. Total the points scored every inning. Play as many innings as time allows.

Additional rules:
• Balls must not be thrown behind the plate or through doorways. Low hanging lights that might obstruct a ball may also be considered out.
• Throwing may be done in any direction, but when the ball is released, the hand must be above the plane of the batter's shoulder. Fielders may not stand directly in front of the batter or hinder the batter in any way.

Phil Blackwell

DUCKBALL

Try this game of kickball with a twist. The pitcher rolls the ball toward the kicker (a one-pitch limit if the group is large), and the kicker kicks away. Before he runs to first base, however, he's handed a fully inflated balloon that he must tuck between his knees and keep there as long as he runs or is on base. Fielders, meanwhile, are also equipped with balloons between their knees (except the pitcher, who cannot assist his team at all) and must waddle as best they can to retrieve the ball and attempt to

put the runners out.

Outs are made touching runners with the ball, either by a tag or a throw. Overthrown balls limit a runner to a single base, as in baseball.

Points are scored by crossing home plate—but that's not the only way. If a fielder pops his balloon, the other team scores a point. Likewise, if a runner pops his balloon, the fielding team scores a point. The game ends when a team earns 20 points or when a predetermined number of innings have been played.

You'll need at least 50 to 60 balloons in a large plastic bag or trash can to begin the game. Use the kids who don't want to play to maintain the balloon supply and to hand balloons to runners on their way to first base.

Variation: If you play Duckball indoors, use a Nerf ball. *Michael W. Capps*

FAT BAT

Here's a version of softball that can be played outdoors in any kind of weather. Anybody can play. It doesn't require much skill.

You'll need to purchase a Fat Bat and Fat Ball from a toy store or department store. They are relatively easy to find and quite inexpensive. Regular softball rules apply, only there are no foul balls. Everything is fair. Players don't use gloves either. The ball is so light that a good wind will carry it all over the place. So, the nastier the weather, the better. *Mark S. Smith*

FRISBALL

This game is played just like softball with any number of players. However, a Frisbee is used instead of a bat and ball. Also, each team gets six outs instead of three. The Frisbee must go at least 30

16

feet on a fly or it is foul. The offensive team does not have to wait until the defensive team is ready before sending their batter to the plate. This keeps the normal between-innings slowdown to a minimum. *Jim Allen*

FUZZYBALL

Here's a take-off on baseball perfect for indoors and for groups of 10 to 50. You'll need a fuzzyball—one of those softball-sized nursery toys with a rubber center and fabric (usually yarn) covering-and a plastic Wiffleball bat. (In a pinch you can use a Nerf ball and a broom.) Lay out home plate and three bases, divide players into two teams, and play ball— well, play fuzzyball.

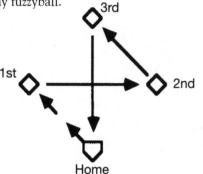

Here are the differences:
• With a hit, players run first to what is normally third base, then to what is normally first base, then to what is normally second base, then home.
• Runners are put out only when tagged by hand or when tagged by the ball below the shoulders. Catching fly balls and tagging bases are not outs.
• Everyone on a team gets to bat once, and only once, each inning, regardless of how many outs. (Outs retire runners from base running; they don't determine the length of the inning.)
• The team at bat supplies its own pitcher. A maximum of three pitches are allowed to each batter. Two strikes constitute an out.

Ralph Gustafson

INNER TUBE BASEBALL

This game is similar to softball, but it utilizes an inner tube. The batter picks up the inner tube at home plate and rotates seven times, heaving the inner tube into the field on the seventh rotation. The batter's

team may count out loud as the batter rotates to help him or her keep track of when to release the tube. Although there are three bases as in softball, there is no out of bounds, so the inner tube may be released in any direction once seven rotations have been completed.

Players are only out when tagged with the inner tube. There are no force outs or pop flies. Defensive players may tag a base runner by touching the runner with the tube or throwing the tube at the runner. Any time the base runner comes in contact with the tube, he is out (unless he is on base, of course).

There is one penalty in this game called "jamming." Jamming occurs when a defensive player tries to cream a base runner with the tube (unnecessary roughness). This is a judgment call on the part of the umpire. Award the offended team with a run and allow the base runner to advance to the closest base. Without this rule some players will attempt to start another game called Maul Ball, which is not recommended for most amateur Inner Tube Baseball players.

The last rule is that the umpire can add or subtract any rules at any time to make the game fun and exciting. All umpire rulings are final unless the umpire receives sufficient financial reimbursement, thus influencing the outcome of the game.

If you wish, have several size inner tubes available so kids can choose a tube appropriate for their size. *Steve Smoker*

KICK THE TIRE

This is simply a game of kickball, using an old fully inflated inner tube instead of a rubber ball. To play, the pitcher rolls the tube up to home plate, where the kicker gives it a swift kick. It may fly, roll, flop, bounce, or whatever. The kicker can be put out by a fly that is caught, or if he is hit with the tube enroute to the base. Or you can have forced outs, just like regular baseball. Whatever rules you decide to use, this variation of an old game is a lot of fun. *Glenn Hermann*

KOOKY KICKBALL

This game can be played on either a baseball diamond or on an open field. Like regular kickball or baseball, one team is up and the other is in the field.

The first batter kicks the ball as it is rolled to him by a teammate. A miss, foul, or ball caught in the air is an out. There are three outs per team per inning. If no outs are made, everyone on the team may go up once during the inning. When the ball is kicked, the fielding team lines up behind the fielder who retrieves the ball. The ball is passed between the legs of all the players from front to rear. The last team member then takes the ball and tags the runner.

Meanwhile, the kickers do not run around the bases. Instead, the team which is up lines up single file behind the batter, who runs around the team as many times as possible. One run is scored for every complete revolution before the batter is tagged with the ball. Play as many innings as you wish. *James Alderson*

KWIFFLE BALL

This fast-paced game combines Kickball and Wiffleball on one baseball diamond.

There are two home plates and two bases. Batters run from home plate (H1) to base A to base B and back to the batter's home plate. Kickers run from the second home plate (H2) to base B to base A and back to the kicker's home plate.

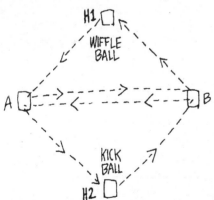

Divide the players into two teams. Team A is split—half go to the Wiffleball home plate and half go to the Kickball home plate. Team B is in the field playing defense against both halves of Team A simultaneously. They have to be alert!

The team that is up provides its own pitchers. Runners from both games can occupy the same base and can be called out by balls (in play) from either game.

Teams switch after the offensive team has a combined three outs from both games. Play a predetermined number of innings. *Jon Bollback*

NERF BASEBALL

This is a great inside winter night activity. All that is needed is a Nerf baseball (three and a half inches in diameter), a plastic bat, and a room large enough for the bases. The bases are 18-inch masking tape squares placed 25 feet apart. The pitcher's mound is about 15 feet from home plate. All the rules are the same as regular baseball except that the runner can be put out if he isn't on the base and is hit by the ball. *Michael Thiel*

NONSTOP CRICKET

I say, how 'bout a game of English nonstop cricket? Using the diagram to guide you, make a bat (or use a similar wooden paddle), make wickets from old broomsticks and a base block, and buy a foam ball. Form two teams of six to 11 participants—the fielders and the players. Choose a wicket keeper from the fielders and a score keeper from among nonplayers (or have a batter record the runs).

The bowler bowls (pitches) with an underhanded throw to the batter, aiming to hit the wicket.

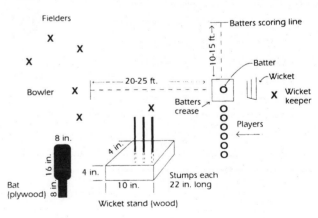

• The batter attempts to hit the ball and on a hit must run and touch the scoring line and return to his crease, so scoring a run.
• The batter is out if the wicket is hit by the bowler, a bowl hits the leg of the batter in front of the wicket, the ball is returned by a fielder and hits the wicket before the batter returns to the crease, or the

wicket keeper hits the wicket with the ball while the batter is out of the crease.

• The batter must run on the third bowl or forfeit a turn.

• The playing field surrounds the batter's crease on all sides.

• Fielders attempt to hit the wicket with the ball directly or through the wicket keeper or bowler. The bowler can bowl whether the batter has returned to the crease or not.

• The entire batting team is out if a fielder catches a fly ball.

Otherwise the batters keep playing until the last batter is out. The batters then become the fielders, and the fielders become the batters. Play for a set time or until an agreed score is reached.

Fred Swallow

OVER THE LINE

Here's a great softball game that is very popular on Southern California beaches. All that is needed is a bat and a softball, six people (three on a team) and some way to mark the boundaries of the playing field, which looks like this:

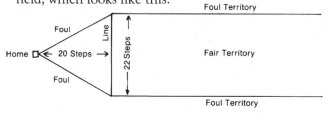

The batter on the team that is up stands at home plate and tries to hit the ball over the line (in the air) into fair territory. The ball is pitched by a teammate about 15 to 20 feet from the batter (anywhere he wants). The pitcher cannot interfere with the ball after it is hit or else the batter is out.

The players in the field position themselves in fair territory (anywhere they want). If they catch a hit ball before it hits the ground, the batter is out. Anything that drops into fair territory on the fly is a base hit. A ball hit in fair territory over the heads of all three fielders is a home run.

There are no bases, so no base running. The bases are imaginary. When a person gets a base hit, the next batter comes up and hits. It takes three base hits (not four as in regular softball) before a run is scored, then every base hit after that adds on

another run. A home run after the first three base hits would score four runs (clearing the bases, plus one bonus run), and it takes three more base hits to start scoring runs again.

Other rules:

• Each batter gets only two pitches to get a hit (only one foul, mis-swing, etc.). If the batter doesn't get a hit in two pitches, he's out.

• Any ball hit on the ground in front of the line is an out (unless it's foul on the first pitch).

• Each team gets three outs per inning, as in regular softball.

• The game is played for nine innings (or as many as you want).

Of course, the rules of the game can be modified as you wish. For example, the boundaries can be adjusted to fit the skills of the players. Or instead of using a softball, you can use a mush ball or a volleyball. You can vary the number of players. It is great on the sand at the beach as well as on a regular playing field.

• **Advanced Over the Line.** Here's a slightly more complicated version of Over the Line. The playing field, the three-person teams, and the other rules remain pretty much the same with a few modifications. The field has two more lines, like so:

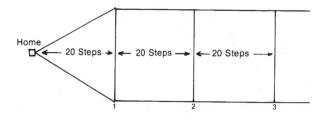

If the batter hits the ball between lines 1 and 2, it's a single; between lines 2 and 3 is a double; over line 3 is a triple, and over the head of the last opposing player is a home run. The defending players can play anywhere they want in the field, but usually it's best to have one player defending each of the three territories.

The scoring is exactly like regular baseball, but all runs must be forced home. For instance, if there is a man on first and second (base runners are still imaginary—nobody really runs) and the next batter hits a double, then one run scores and now there are men on second and third. If the next guy hits a single, nobody scores since first base is open. Another single would score a run, since the bases are loaded.

Singles, doubles, and triples are usually only counted as such when the ball crosses the appropriate line in the air. However, for more excitement and larger scores, it can be done this way: A single must land behind line 1 on the fly (as usual), but if the fielder lets it roll or bounce past line 2 in fair territory, then it is a double, even though it hit the ground in single territory. Same thing with a triple. If the ball crosses the third line, no matter how it got there, it goes as a triple. Home runs are still the same—over the head of everybody. All other rules are the same as regular Over the Line.

PARACHUTE KICKBALL

Mark off a 100-foot square in the church parking lot or in a field. Divide players into two teams. One team stands within the square, each helping to hold a parachute or large sheet. The other team stands outside the square, either scattered around it or together in a line; this team has a soccer or playground ball.

The object for the outside team is to take turns kicking the ball with a high, arching kick that lands within the square. If the ball lands within the square and is not caught by the parachute, the kicking team gets a point. If the ball is caught by the parachute, or if the kicked ball lands outside the square, or if the kick is judged to be insufficiently high or arching—then an out is called against the kicking team. Like baseball, teams trade places after three outs. *David Shaw*

PEW BALL

If the weather outside is the pits and your church has no gym, try playing this game in your church sanctuary. Use the center aisle for the base-running path, and fielders can position themselves among the pews. Depending on the size of the sanctuary and the vulnerability of stained-glass windows, sound systems, and the like, you may want to use a large Nerf ball instead of a volleyball. *Roger Rome*

PLUNGER BALL

Here's another great variation of baseball your kids will love. To play, you need a large rubber or plastic ball (not too heavy) and a good old American toilet plunger. This game can be played indoors or out.

Divide into two teams. One team is in the field and the other is at bat. The team that is up bats with the plunger by poking at the ball with the rubber part on the end. The runner runs to first, and all the normal rules of baseball or softball apply.

You can change the rules as you see fit. For example, it's usually best to have four or five bases rather than the customary three. They can also be closer together. Boundaries can be adjusted and positions in the field can be created spontaneously. Players can be put out by hitting them with the ball. You can have five outs per inning, rather than three. *Lee Strawhun*

POLISH BASEBALL

This is a great game for groups of 50 or more (25 per team). There are only two bases: home plate and first base (located approximately 120 feet from home). A regular baseball bat is used with a slightly mushy volleyball. There is no out-of-bounds. The ball can be hit in any direction. The pitcher is from the team that is batting. Each

batter gets only one pitch. The batter does not have to accept the pitch, but if he does swing, it counts as one pitch. Outs are made in the following manner:

• A missed swing
• A fly ball that is caught
• A force out at first base
• Being touched by the ball

Players cannot be forced out at home. Runners can be hit by a thrown ball or tagged out.

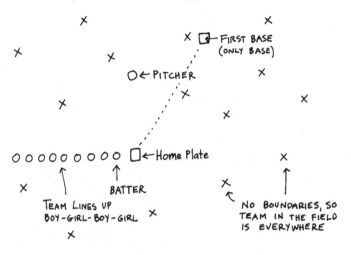

Once a runner reaches the first base, he does not have to leave until it's safe to. Any amount of players can be on first base at the same time. As soon as the teams switch. The batting team does not have to wait for the fielding team to get in position as long as all of their players are lined up behind home.

You can have up to four games going at once, on the same field but on different sides of the field, which can be very confusing, but a lot of fun. Each game needs a neutral umpire who judges outs. The team with the most runs wins. Any amount of innings can be played.

• **Crock Ball.** For variation, play Crock Ball, which involves the use of a two-foot high wastebasket (the crock). There are also a few rule changes. The wastebasket is turned upside down and acts as home plate. First base is 30 to 40 feet away from home plate, and there are no other bases. The playing field is 360 degrees around home base. In other words, there are no foul areas. A pitcher's mound is placed about 20 feet from home.

The batter may use any type of a bat and must hit the ball (a large playground ball or volleyball, slightly deflated) so that it does not knock over the crock. After hitting the ball, the

batter must run to first base, then return to home base to score a run. The opposing players must chase down the ball and throw it to the pitcher, who must knock over the crock to make an out. One person can score several runs by herself—if she hits a long ball, she may run from home to first several times.

Change pitchers every inning so that one person does not dominate the game. The pitch must be lobbed underhand up over the crock, and the batter may wait for a pitch that's in the strike zone. If the pitcher knocks over the crock, then a run is scored for the at-bat team. An umpire is optional. Once the batter swings, the ball is in play, even if he misses. The only way to get the batter out is to knock over the crock, even on fly balls that are caught in the air. (Although if you have hard hitters that consistently hit the ball for distance, you could count caught flies as outs. It forces them to get it on the ground.)

• **Obstacle Ball.** When a sudden rainstorm threatens to dampen your recreational spirit, retreat indoors to a large room for this variation of Polish Baseball. Leaving a clear running lane between home plate and first base, litter the field liberally with folding chairs or other obstacles—this way a hit ball won't travel very far. It'll ricochet off or roll under a chair where it's hard to get to. Throws to put out runners will be deflected. *George Wood and Vernon Edington*

SCORE BALL

This variation of baseball is a great equalizer of talent—nonathletic types do as well as your group's jocks. All you need is an indoor or outdoor playing area marked into zones (see diagram), a bat, and three differently colored Nerf balls.

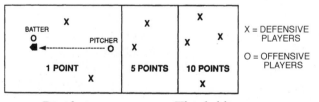

Divide into two teams. The fielding team spreads out in the "field" while the team at bat sends its first member to the plate to hit. Here's how to play:

A batter gets only three pitches; three strikes put him out, as does a fly ball that a fielder catches.

The three colored balls are pitched in the same sequence for each batter. Here's why: The first pitch (say, the red ball) is worth one point if it's hit; the second (yellow), two points; the third (blue), three points. Colored balls make it easy to keep track of the points. So a batter may choose either to hit whatever ball comes his way or to wait for the second or third pitch for more points.

There's more—the point value of a hit ball is multiplied by the point value of the zone it lands in.

For example, if the batter hits the second pitch (two points) into the middle zone (five points), she earns 10 points for her team. A hit, therefore, can earn anywhere from one to 30 points.

Play as many innings as you like! *Roger Rome*

SIAMESE SOFTBALL

This is a perfect game for a group too large to play a regular softball game. Teams are evenly divided and team members are paired by hooking their arms together. At no time while playing are they allowed to unhook their arms or use their hooked arms. They may use their free arms and hands. A rubber ball or volleyball is used instead of a softball because it can be caught with the pair's free arms and hands. Only one person needs to throw the ball.

When at bat, pairs are to grasp the bat with their free hands together. After the ball is hit, the pair must run the bases with arms hooked together. Other than these exceptions everything else is played with regular softball rules. *Michael Allen*

SOCK BALL

This version of softball can be played with regular softball rules. It can be played indoors because you play the game with socks. Everything is made out of socks. Stuff a large sock full of socks to make a sock bat; make a ball the same way. No shoes are allowed during the game; only socks. On a freshly waxed floor, this game can be a hoot. *Louise and Jim Warnock*

SWEDISH BASEBALL

This variation of baseball is most effective with 25 or more participants. Teams are divided equally with one team out in the field and the other at bat. No bats or balls are used. All you need is a Frisbee.

The batter comes to the plate and throws the Frisbee out into the field. The fielding team chases down the Frisbee and tries to return it to a garbage can that is next to home plate. The Frisbee must be tossed in rather than simply dropped in. Meanwhile, the batter runs about 10 feet to the first base, then

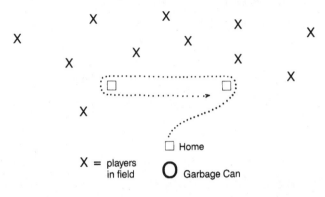

X = players in field
□ Home
O Garbage Can

to the second base about eight feet away and begins to circle them. Every lap is one point for the batting team, and the runner continues until the Frisbee is in the can. All the players on the batting team get to be up each inning. There are no outs.

After two or three innings, the score can get quite high. You'll need to have a scorekeeper who can keep track of all the points. *David Rasmussen*

TARZAN KICKBALL

Jazz up traditional kickball by setting up a portable sound system and playing background music of prerecorded bits of fast-moving, motion-picture soundtracks. You can also throw in some lively old stuff like "Oklahoma!" Your local library is a good resource for music. As you're making the tape, every once in a while dub in a Tarzan yell (also from the library). The cassette should run about 35 minutes, with 10 to 15 Tarzan yells interspersed throughout the recording.

With the music playing in the background, play regulation kickball, with the following addition: When players hear the Tarzan yell, they must immediately stop playing, no matter what the action is. The kicking team must run to their team base in center field and squat down, while the fielding team runs to their team base behind home plate and squats down.

Making the teams run through each other to get to their base adds to the excitement of the game.

The first team all together and squatting down receives 10 points.

Once the winner is determined for that yell, normal play resumes exactly where it left off. Runners return to their positions on the bases, and the ball is returned to whomever had it at the time of the yell. Runs are scored as usual. The team with the most runs at the end of the time period wins.

To play longer than 35 minutes, just rewind the tape. Assign a judge to say which team is first to be all together and squatting after the yell.

For a variation let each team bat once through the lineup, then switch to outfield.

Rich Cooper and Tim Maughan

THREE BALL

Here's a great outdoor game from New Zealand that can be used with almost any age group and any number of people. You need a baseball diamond (or a reasonable facsimile) and three balls of any kind. You can use softballs, footballs, rugby balls, soccer balls, volleyballs, or just about anything that can be thrown. You can use Frisbees, if you want to. The three balls you use don't have to be the same, either. You also need a cardboard box, trash can, bucket, or something that the balls can go in.

The box (for the balls) sits at home plate. One team is up and the other team is out in the field, just like regular baseball. There are no positions, however. Everybody just plays everywhere. The first batter at the plate selects three balls (if there are more to choose from). He then must get rid of all three of them as quickly as possible, any way he wants to—by kicking, throwing, etc. The balls must stay within the boundaries of the field.

After getting rid of the balls, he starts running the bases while the team in the field tries to return all three balls back to the box at home plate. The player who is running the bases gets a point for each base he reaches before the balls are back in the box and five bonus points if he makes it all the way around. If a ball is caught on the fly, then that ball does not have to be placed in the box—it is dead. If the runner is caught between bases when the last of the three balls are placed in the box, then he loses all his accumulated points. He must watch and stop so that he is safely on a base when all the balls are finally in.

There are no outs. The best way to play is to let everyone on the team have a chance each inning and just add up the total points scored. When everybody has had a turn, the other team is up. You can play as many innings as you want. If you have larger groups, then get several games going at once. It doesn't matter if the fields overlap.

Since it is very easy to get to first base (at least), it means that everyone can contribute to the team score and have fun. You will need one referee for the game to blow the whistle (or whatever) when the balls come in and to help keep score. Boundaries, distance between the bases, etc., can be adjusted depending on the size and skill of the group.

The Campus Life Staff, New Plymouth, New Zealand

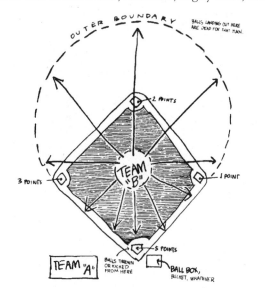

WALL BASEBALL

During lock-ins, retreats, or any other times that find you indoors, Wall Baseball is safe, fun, and doesn't require typical baseball skills in order for kids of any age to have fun playing it. Here's what you'll need: a wall (preferably 15x10 feet, though any size will do), masking tape, labels, and a Ping-Pong ball and paddle. Use the masking tape and labels to duplicate this diagram on your wall:

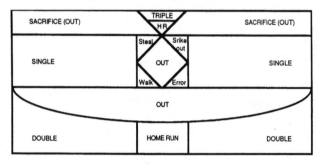

Lay a home plate on the floor 20 feet or so away from the wall and a pitching rubber halfway or so between the wall and home plate.

Now to play. The pitcher tosses the Ping-Pong ball to the batter, who attempts to hit it with the paddle toward the wall. Where the ball hits the wall determines the play. If the ball hits the single area, for example, then the batter has hit a single and may proceed to first base. Defensive players position themselves wherever they think they can catch fly balls or prevent balls from hitting the game wall.

Other rules:
• All players—pitcher, batter, everyone—play on their knees at all times.
• Balls that hit the floor or ceiling before hitting the wall are ruled as outs.
• There's no base running necessary in this game—all outs are force outs. Runners (so to speak) advance around the bases on their knees, and consequently very slowly.

• No fast pitching.

A plate ump is usually a good idea for calling obvious strikes and deciding where on the wall the ball hits in the case of a dispute. Play as many innings as you want. *Brett C. Wilson*

WRONG WAY BASEBALL

This is an indoor or outdoor version of baseball, depending on the size of the group and your facilities. Play follows the standard rules, except that alternating batters run opposite directions around the bases when they get a hit.

For instance, Batter 1 gets a hit, so she runs as usual to first base on a single. Then Batter 2 gets a hit; he runs the opposite way—to third base—and so clockwise around the diamond. The catch, of course, is when two base runners are approaching the same base from different directions. If both arrive on the same base at the end of a play, they're both out.

Hilarious antics follow when kids realize they haven't thought ahead to what may happen next if they continue their course without cooperation. The team in the field must also talk to each other more to keep up with where the best plays are. (Do we smell a teachable moment here?)

Some details:
• A hitter who runs the wrong direction must first return to and touch home plate before running to the appropriate base.
• The direction hitters run is based on batting order, not hitting order. In other words, odd-numbered batters (not hitters) run the bases normally; even-numbered batters, if they get a hit, run the bases clockwise.
• In a gymnasium or large room, use a Whiffleball and bat. Fly balls caught after ricocheting off a wall or ceiling are not outs.

Kent Taylor

FOOTBALL
GAMES

Here's your autumn outdoor game list! Some of these ideas are slight variations of traditional football; others are fullblown overhauls of gridiron action. Hilarity ensues when you replace the old pigskin with a tennis ball, a Trac-Ball—even a teddy bear! All the fun of football (though without the sensation of a 300-pound lineman belly-flopping onto your prone body).

FEATHER FOOTBALL

Divide the group into teams of about six people each, and mark goal lines at each end of the room and a center line down the middle. Place one team in each half of the room, and ask them to get down on their hands and knees. Place a feather on the center line between the two teams, and on a signal each team tries to blow the feather across its goal line. Have the winners of the first game compete with the next team and so on. *Randall Newburn*

BLIND FOOTBALL

This is a rough but fun game that can only be played in a room without furniture. Use a ball that can be easily held on to (deflated volleyball, etc.) but which is indestructible. The object of the game is for one team to touch the ball to the wall on its opponent's side of the room.

Throw the ball into the middle of the room and just as the two teams start to fight over it, turn off the lights. From that point until a team scores, turn on the light only every 30 seconds or so. Instruct the players to freeze in position when the lights come on. Leave the light on for just a few seconds so they can see who has the ball, then turn the lights back off. The positions the guys get into in the dark is hilarious. It is recommended that girls play separately from the guys so they are less likely to get hit as hard and also because clothing can become disheveled, making for some very embarrassing moments when the lights are turned back on. *Gary Sumner*

CAPTURE THE FOOTBALL

This game is based on Capture the Flag (see page xx), but instead of using flags, use footballs. It can be played by smaller groups with less room as well as large groups. Also, it doesn't have to be completely dark.

Footballs are placed in each team's territory. You must get the other team's football over to your team's territory. You may pass the ball over the line to win or run it over. If players are tagged, they must remain a prisoner until a teammate tags them. If the ball is passed to a teammate over the line that separates the team territories and the receiver drops it, both become prisoners. If the pass is complete, that team wins. Adapt the rest of the standard Capture the Flag rules to your group and setting for the best results. *Larry Jansen*

FIELD HANDBALL

For this football-soccer hybrid, you'll need a large ball (soccer ball, football, volleyball—even a playground ball will do), two durable chairs, and tape or spray paint or rope to mark off the goal circles. Pylons to mark the field boundaries and armbands to distinguish teams are optional.

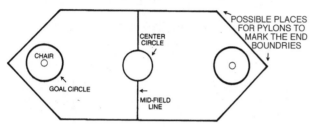

The goal of play is simply to hit the opponent's chair—which sits in the center of a 12-foot-diameter goal circle at the end of the field—with the ball.

Here's how to play:
• You may run with the ball or pass the ball to a teammate.
• If a ball runner is tagged, she has three seconds to pass the ball to a teammate; otherwise, the other team takes possession on the spot. A goal cannot be scored during these three seconds.
• If a player drops a pass from a teammate, any opponent picks up the ball and continues play. An intercepted pass is also played without a break.
• No one, defender or attacker, may enter either of the goal circles. Otherwise, the ball changes possession and play is renewed at the nearest boundary line.
• Following a goal, play begins again in the center circle as in soccer.

You may want to use a referee, especially to curtail unnecessary roughness. The referee can impose a loss-of-possession penalty or temporary suspension from the game. *Mark E. Byers*

FLAMINGO FOOTBALL

Announce that you are going to play tackle football with the guys playing against the girls. This idea sounds great to the guys until they learn that they must play with a handicap. Guys must tackle, run, pass, hike, catch, and kick while holding one foot off the ground with one hand. The girls love it.

FOOTBALL FRENZY

Divide into two teams and divide your playing field in half. The game starts with each team occupying only their half of the field. Each team gets a football. The object is for a player on each team to hike its ball to a second teammate who attempts to pass the ball to any other teammate in the opposition's territory within 30 seconds. The referee starts the action by blowing a whistle, keeps time, and blows the whistle when time has expired. If the pass is intercepted, the defending team gets six points. If the pass is completed, the passing team gets seven points. If the pass falls incomplete, the defending team gets one point.

With both teams trying to complete passes, the teams are on offense and defense at the same time. To make sure the jocks don't monopolize the game, make a rule that no one may be quarterback or may catch a pass more than once per game or per quarter. Play four quarters of five minutes each (10 pass attempts). After each pass, players must return to their side of the field. The game is a lot of fun, and once the kids get the hang of it, they'll want to play it often. *Bill Rudge*

JUNGLE FOOTBALL

This is essentially touch or flag football. However, all players are eligible to catch a pass. The quarterback or ball carrier can also run across the line of scrimmage and still pass the ball in any direction, to another player. Multiple passes are allowed on one play. Each team gets four downs to score. There aren't any first downs. Only touchdowns are counted (six points) and safeties (two points). The rules can be changed or modified to fit any size group, age, sex, etc. Have your own Jungle Football Super Bowl! *Ray Kelle*

MIDNIGHT FOOTBALL

This rowdy game is great for boys of all ages,

although it can also be played with girls. It is played indoors in a room or hallway that is relatively free of furniture, and which can be made pitch dark. Then you need two teams and an eraser for the football.

To begin, teams line up against opposing walls. Players on both teams are on their hands and knees. The lights go out and one team kicks off by sliding the eraser over to the other team. A brief time is allowed for the receiving team to make any hand-offs they want, and then play begins. The team that kicked off goes out to meet the opposing team in the dark and attempts to stop it from scoring by searching every person.

Scoring is accomplished by successfully crossing the room with the eraser and touching the opposite wall with it. Teams are permitted to pass the eraser, but players need to be sneaky and careful or they will lose it to the opposition. The eraser must be carried by hand across the room. No stuffing it inside clothing. Players must also remain on their hands and knees during the active play.

If there is a fumble or an interception (the kicking team somehow manages to capture the eraser), then play is stopped and the teams line up again at opposing walls. The team that recovered the eraser now becomes the receiving team.

Michael McKnight

Nerf Football League

Now your youth group can have its very own NFL. This crazy version of football can be played indoors with almost any number of kids. You could divide into teams and have a Nerf Football Tournament, with the Super Bowl as its climax. Here's the way the game is played:

• Basic football rules are in force. The object is to score touchdowns. The football field should be marked with boundaries, goal lines, etc.

• There is absolutely no running or fast walking allowed. The officials can determine penalties for this. All players must walk when the ball is in play.

• There are only four downs allowed. No first downs. If you can't score a touchdown in four attempts, then the ball is turned over to the other team.

• Passing can be in any direction to any player on the same team. There can be more than one pass per

down. In other words, players can keep passing the ball until someone is finally tagged by an opposing player.

• No tackling. This should be two-hand touch or flag football.

• Don't replay interference calls. Low ceilings, furniture, etc., are all part of the game. Adapt the

• The ball must be a soft, spongy Nerf ball or something similar.

Jeff Dietrich

Pigskin Prognosticators

Get your kids into Sunday school—and on time, at that—by holding a contest in which they try to predict the winners of each week's NFL games. Girls enjoy the opportunity to show up guys who think they know a lot about football—and since the element of luck is great, this happens often. Divide the season into four four-game quarters and offer a prize to the premier prognosticator for each quarter.

Byron D. Harvey

Play in the Dark

For nighttime football, make a hole in a Nerf ball and push a Cyalume glow stick into the end of the ball. Point the lighted end toward the receiver for passing downs. Or attach a Cyalume glow stick to a Frisbee to play Frisbee in the dark. *Larry Smith*

Teddy Bear Football

Although this game sounds corny, a little hype and the right mix of humor makes this flag-football perversion more than bearable. In fact, it's actually become an annual event at one church, drawing players and spectators alike.

It's traditional flag football, though played in a gym or fellowship hall—and with a teddy bear instead of a football.

In a gym roomy enough for running, passing, and—yes—kicking a teddy bear, erect goal posts from two-by-fours, or use crepe paper taped to the walls for field-goal markers. In a short gym, for instance, allow only five downs. If the team does not score, it must punt the bear to the other team or try for a field goal on the fifth down. (Be sure to use traditional punting and kicking formations.) You may want to include a girls-only quarter, followed by a boys-only quarter. During the remaining quarters, keep the girls active by requiring that a girl touch the ball once during each possession. In coed teams, of course, limit the physical contact involved in blocking or running over people.

A 15-inch bear is just the right size; it will work well for kickoffs, passes, punts, and field goals. (The smaller stuffed bears just don't provide the same level of sadistic pleasure.) KIPP Brothers sells reasonably priced carnival bears (800/428-1153 or 317/634-5507). You may be able to borrow a bear, but the likelihood of returning it the way you received it is slim. In fact, you'll probably need a replacement bear to finish off the game—so get two.

Cue the referee to use creative calls like "Roughing the teddy!" Then play traditional flag football, modifying the rules to fit your situation.

Half-time? Offer a refreshment stand (free snacks), a kazoo marching band, and the crowning of a queen (a guy dressed up like a girl). *Steve Smoker*

TOUCHDOWN TENNIS

This game is touch football with tennis rackets and tennis balls. The quarterback uses a tennis racket; the ball is centered to the quarterback who hits the ball to any teammate. Regular rules of touch football apply. A player can only catch one pass in a series of downs and three completed passes make a first down. Kickoffs are done with the tennis racket. Defense players may rush only after counting to 10. The racket cannot be exchanged during a play.

Chuck Williams

TRAC-BALL TOURNEY

Here are two games—an outdoor field game and an indoor gym game—that use Trac-Ball scoops—something like the Mexican jai alai. You can pick up a Wham-O Trac-Ball set (two scoops and a ball or two) from most department, toy, or sporting-goods stores.

• **Trac Football.** Remember the variation of football called Speedball or Razzle Dazzle Touch Football—where the quarterback must pass, and then receivers themselves can pass anywhere on the field in order to move the ball toward the goal? Play with Trac-Ball scoops and a Trac-Ball ball—and you've got Trac Football. Only three rules:

1. Play is dead not by touching or tackling the ball carrier, but when the ball touches the ground. Defensive strategy, then, calls for interfering with a throw or a reception and trying to knock the ball from a carrier's scoop. A team gets four downs in which to score. (See rule 3 about first downs.)

2. The ball is advanced only by throwing it, not by running it. A player may scramble behind the line of scrimmage (the point at which the play begins, or the point at which a receiver catches the ball), but a ball carrier may not run beyond the line of scrimmage until he hurls the ball. Teammates (potential receivers) may run anywhere, of course.

3. Two complete passes earn a first down. Those passes may come within a single play, or one may occur in one down, the other during another down. Any time during the four downs that a team completes its second pass, it earns a first down. (If your group gets good at Trac Football, increase the difficulty of earning first downs: Require three completes for a first, award two consecutive first downs if a team completes three passes within a single play, etc.)

Interceptions, kickoffs, hikes, punts—they're all done similarly to regular touch football, but within the limitations imposed by these three rules.

Six scoops may be a minimum amount of equipment to start out with. Some Trac Football players don't think a maximum exists. "The more, the better!" they say.

• **Macho Trac-Ball.** This lacrosse-like game will become a favorite of the rough-and-tough guys in your group. Situate two equal teams of any size on opposite sides of a center line. Now supply indoor hockey nets at either end (or draw or tape an area on the two opposite baseline walls, or simply use the closed gym doors as goals if they are at the proper ends of the gym).

Equip players with two balls and at least six Trac-Ball scoops. The object of the contest is to hurl a ball into the opponent's goal—but at no time can players cross the center line into their opponents' side. Teams may defend their goals by putting as many of their players as they want in front of the goals. In so doing, they'll get stung a bit by balls flung at their goal, but they'll also be thwarting attempts on their goal by the opposition across the center line.

The twist to this dodging game is the spin that Trac-Ball scoops put on the ball. It's hard to judge curves coming at you 60 miles per hour. *Dik LaPine*

ULTIMATE FOOTBALL

Guaranteed to tire the most rambunctious junior high boys, this game requires only a Frisbee and lets everyone play quarterback and receiver.

Play on a football-type field with goal lines at either end. The object is to cross the goal line with a Frisbee. Play consists not in running (yet), but in passing the Frisbee in order to move it downfield.

Here's the shift to football: If the Frisbee holder does not throw it by the time a covering opponent counts to 10, the Frisbee holder is free to run with the Frisbee—and also free to be tackled by the opposing team if he does not throw on the run to a teammate. The Frisbee changes teams in the case of a tackle, an interception, or an incomplete pass.

Needless to say, your junior high boys will get their fill of tackling and running with this game! *John Krienke*

FRISBEE
GAMES

Portable, readily available in most homes, and supremely cool.
The fabulous flying Frisbee disc can provide hours of entertainment for
your group members. In fact, why not plan an entire day of Frisbee games?
Plenty of ideas here to choose from.

CROSBEE

This game is a mixture of Frisbee and lacrosse. All that is needed is a playing field, a Frisbee, and 10 to 75 kids. Goals are set up on opposite ends of the field. Use two markers about 10 feet apart. Divide up into two teams. Each team selects goalies and perhaps other positions such as defense, offense, forward, middle, back, etc.

The two teams then line up on opposite ends of the field and the Frisbee is placed in the middle. On the starting whistle, players go for the Frisbee, and the first to get it may pass it to any other player on the team. When a player catches it, he may run with it, pass it, or down it, which is a stop. (To down it, he simply falls on it.) Any player carrying the Frisbee may be tagged by a member of the other team and must then surrender the Frisbee to the opponent immediately. Referees make judgments on this. If a player downs the Frisbee before being tagged, she can then stand up and throw it to any other player on the team without interference. However, once the Frisbee is thrown, it may be intercepted. Also, a person downing the Frisbee cannot score after downing it. Goals are scored by throwing the Frisbee between the goals. *Whitey White*

FRISBEE ATTACK

Here's an exciting version of Frisbee Tag. To play, you'll need a playing area with a radius of about 40 feet. The game is best played with five to 10 players. One person is chosen to be "It," and another is chosen to be the Frisbee thrower. "It" is free to move around, while the Frisbee thrower must stand in the middle of the bounded area, preferably on a chair or table. You will need at least three Frisbees (or other flying discs).

The object of the game is for "It" to get the other players out by hitting them with a Frisbee. As the game begins, "It" has all the Frisbees in his or her possession and tries to hit the other players with them. If a player is hit, he or she is frozen and can no longer move. If "It" misses, the Frisbee can be captured by anyone who wants to run after it. When a Frisbee is captured, the player who has it can try to get it to the Frisbee thrower in the middle of the field, either by carrying it or throwing it. This is important, because only the Frisbee thrower is able to unfreeze players who have been frozen by "It." The Frisbee thrower accomplishes this by throwing a Frisbee to one of the frozen players, who must catch it before it hits the ground. In catching the

Frisbee, the frozen player may only move one foot. If he or she moves both feet, the throw is invalid. If the player becomes unfrozen, he or she may give the Frisbee back to the Frisbee thrower to release another frozen player.

Meanwhile, "It" is still scrambling around trying to hit players with Frisbees, intercept captured Frisbees, and so on. The game ends when "It" has frozen everyone and the Frisbee thrower has no more Frisbees to throw. As more players are added, more "Its" can also be added. It's not too difficult to find the right balance so that the competition stays even.

Allow everyone a chance to be "It," and give a prize to the one who can freeze everyone in the game in the shortest time. You might want to set a time limit for each "It." *Harold Atterlei and Dan Young*

Frisbee Bowling

A number of people can play this game, and very little skill is required. To set up, all you need is a table, 10 paper cups, and three Frisbees or other flying discs. The cups are stacked in a pyramid several inches away from the far edge of the table. From a distance of about 20 feet, each player gets three attempts to knock as many of the cups as possible onto the floor, by hitting them with the Frisbee.

Each cup is worth one point. You can call each round a frame as in regular bowling, with a game consisting of as many frames as you like. If more than five people are playing, keep a pencil and paper handy to keep track of the score. To keep the game moving, players can take turns throwing the Frisbees, retrieving them, and restacking the paper cups. *Deborah Cusson and Sean Mahar*

Frisbee Bull's-Eye

Add this to an afternoon of Frisbee mania. This two-part game works best with 30 kids or more. Divide them into three or four teams, then announce the first part: competition in a stated game (it doesn't matter what game) in order to earn Frisbees. First place is awarded five Frisbees; second place, three Frisbees; third place, two; and fourth place, one.

Now for part two: Each team appoints a thrower, who is entrusted with floating his team's Frisbees onto a horizontal target from behind a line 20 feet or so away from the target. The target can simply be three concentric circles—throwers score 10 points for their team if a Frisbee lands within the innermost circle, five points within the next circle, and one point if within the outside circle.

Teams can play as many rounds of this as they like, giving most of a team's players the chance to be thrower. *Randy Hausler*

Frisbee Golf

Lay out a short golf course around the area using telephone poles, light posts, fence posts, tree trunks, etc., for holes. You can set up places as the tees or designate a certain distance from the previous hole (such as 10 feet) for the starting place. Each person needs a Frisbee. The object of the game is to take as few throws as possible to hit all the holes. Each person takes his first throw from the tee and then stands where it landed for his next throw until he hits the hole. Of course discretion must be used when the Frisbee lands in a bush or tree. One penalty throw is added to the score if the Frisbee can't be thrown from where it lands.

The course can be as simple or as complicated as the skill of the participants warrants. Such things as doglegs, doorways, arches, and narrow fairways add to the fun of the course. Take three or four good Frisbee throwers through the course to set the par for each hole. It is a good test of skill, but anybody can do it.

Two other games for a Frisbee Night could include a distance throw and an accuracy throw (like through a Hula Hoop from 30 feet).

• **Glow-in-the-Dark Frisbee Golf.** Here's a great variation of the standard Frisbee golf game! Provide two or three glow-in-the-dark Frisbees. You can purchase them at many sports shops for around $10 each. Set up a Frisbee course by cutting out cardboard to form several hollow rings large enough for a Frisbee to pass through. Paint lines on the rings with glow-in-the-dark paint that can be purchased at craft stores. Paint numbers on other pieces of cardboard to designate each hole, and decide on an appropriate par. Divide into teams and compete for the lowest team score.

• **Indoor Frisbee Miniature Golf.** In an appropriate section of the church building (nowhere near stained glass), set up an indoor course, labeling as holes trash cans, teachers' podiums, chairs, doors, and so on. You can also use shoe boxes or 8½ x 11 sheets of paper as the holes.

Reproduce the master scorecard with rules and a blank list of the 18 holes (page 38). On the master, fill in the holes. For example:

Hole 1—Trash can by phone
Hole 2—Music, Room 201
Hole 3—Library, Room 2
Hole 4—Second grade, Room 3
Hole 5—Nursery, Room 4
Hole 6—Fifth/sixth grade, Room 5

Then photocopy enough scorecards for all your Frisbee golfers.

For the Frisbees, gather 30 or more lids from five-pound cottage-cheese containers or similar six-inch disks. The lids are small enough to be unable to break anything, but large enough to be thrown with at least some accuracy. Number the lids so the kids can tell which is theirs. Explain the rules that are printed on the scorecard, then start each team in a different location, so that they can all start and finish at about the same time.

Once you collect the parts for this game, keep cards and lids on hand for that moment when the VCR eats your evening's tape. It's a great spur-of-the-moment lifesaver. *Jim Berkley, Leif A. Ford, and* **Kevin Bueltmann**

FRISBEE INSANITY

Divide your group into three teams and have them stand in a circle with two to three feet between players. Everyone should be standing next to one member from each of the other two teams. Give each team a Frisbee. Players only throw to the other members of the same team. At the signal all teams throw simultaneously, trying to get as many catches as possible in a two-minute period. Prohibit players from throwing to the nearest teammates to the left and right. The team with the most catches wins.

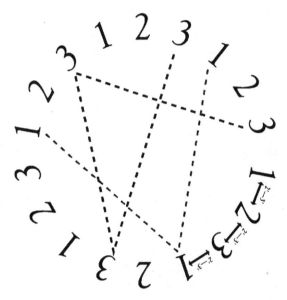

For variety, you can give each team two Frisbees, or place one member from each team within the circle to deflect the throws of opposing teams, or both.

Soft Frisbees made out of heavy material work best. They fly wonderfully and virtually negate the possibility of injury. You can find them at many toy stores, or "Soft Flight" Frisbees can be ordered from Project Adventure, Inc., P.O. Box 100, Hamilton, MA 01936, 508/468-7981, for around $10. *Jeff Crosby*

FRISBEE RUGBY

Divide your group into two teams (this game is played best with 25 or less players). Set up goals at opposite ends of the field. Team A tries to advance the Frisbee over one goal line while Team B tries to advance the Frisbee over the opposite goal line. A Frisbee can only be advanced by throwing it to a

INDOOR FRISBEE MINIATURE GOLF RULES

- Golf teams are 2 to 4 players.
- Stay with your group, and don't run around wildly.
- At each hole take turns throwing your first putt. The player closest to the hole finishes his turn, followed by the player next closest to the hole, and so on.
- Keep track (honestly) of how many throws it takes to make your putt. Record that score in the appropriate box. (Lowest score wins.)
- You must be within three feet of the previous hole when you start throwing to the next.
- You may not stop a Frisbee that is moving or rolling.
- Except for when you tee off, one foot must touch the spot where the Frisbee lands when you throw it.
- Each team decides at the beginning if it will use Pro Rules (the Frisbee must land inside the trash can) or Beginner Rules (the Frisbee need only hit the can).
- It is polite for a slower team to allow a faster team to pass it. It is not polite for a faster team to interfere with a slower team's game.
- All holes are trash cans, except where noted otherwise.
- Par is four on all holes (72 total).
- Have fun, but don't destroy the building in the process.

Hole

1

2

3

4

5

6

7

8

9

10

11

12

13

14

15

16

17

18

teammate. Each person can only take three steps before throwing the Frisbee. If they take more than three steps, the Frisbee goes to the opposite team. A person must be allowed five seconds to throw the Frisbee without harassment; if they wait longer, they can be blitzed by their opponents. If the Frisbee is dropped, or if it hits the ground before being caught, the team that had possession last must give it over to the opposing team.

• **Soccerfriz.** Or try this variation. Divide your group into three to seven teams of five to 15 people each. Each team should have some kind of identifying mark, such as a colored wristband or tie. Next have each team mark a goal—a circle on the ground about three yards across. Each goal should be 20 yards or so from the center of the field and equidistant from the others.

The object of the game is for each team to get as many Frisbees as possible into its own goal and to prevent Frisbees from going into other goals. The referee starts the action by throwing a Frisbee into the group, and players take it from there. More Frisbees can be added when players get the hang of the game. The more the better. Once a Frisbee is in a goal, it is dead and stays there until all Frisbees are down and that round is over.

Here are the rules:

• Frisbees may only be thrown, kicked, or rolled. They cannot be carried—you may move only one step when you throw.

• People who have Frisbees in their possession cannot be touched, only guarded.

• Frisbees may not be grabbed from anyone.

• If two people catch one at once, the boy must give it up to the girl and the larger person must give it up to the smaller person.

• Players who break the rules must sit out of the game for three minutes.

Marshall Shelley and Alan C. Wilder

FRISBEE SWAT

What you'll need for this active game are two (or more) Frisbees, two chairs, two cones (or liter bottles), two teams, and a rolled up newspaper for each player. At each end of the playing area, place a chair with a cone on its seat. The purpose is for each team to knock the other team's cone off the chair with a Frisbee. Points are awarded for each knockdown.

Team members pass the Frisbees to each other as they work their way down the field. No one is allowed to run with the Frisbee—they can only pass it. Team members hold a newspaper in one hand, which is used for knocking down the opponent's Frisbee, and use their other hand to catch and throw their team's Frisbee. To play the game teams must attempt to score on offense and at the same time maneuver around on defense to swat the opponent's Frisbee out of the air. *Ed Martinez*

FRISBEE TIMER TAG

On a large, flat playing field with clearly marked boundaries, divide players into two teams. Each team's members decide how long they think they can keep possession of the Frisbee.

Then teams gather near the center for the toss out: The referee-timer throws the Frisbee into any part of the field to begin the game. The clock begins when a player touches the Frisbee and continues until the player with the Frisbee is tagged or the Frisbee touches the ground. Players may run with the Frisbee or throw it to another team member. The offensive team's captain yells out the estimated time and keeps up with points.

Scoring: A team receives points when it retains possession of the Frisbee for the amount of seconds the members estimated. Points received are equal to the number of seconds the team members estimated they could possess the Frisbee.

Turnovers: A team relinquishes possession of the Frisbee to their opponents when—

• The Frisbee touches the ground.

• The Frisbee or the player possessing it goes out of bounds.

• The player with the Frisbee is tagged by an opponent.

• The player with the Frisbee runs out of bounds to avoid being tagged.

After a period of play, let teams make new estimates of their possession time before resuming the game. *Greg Miller*

KILLER FRISBEE

Form a circle, spacing people so there is enough room to roam in the middle, but not so much that players are able to remain in the center indefinitely. The object is to try to remain in the center of the circle while the others try to hit the player in the middle with a Frisbee. The person must be hit below the shoulders. Use a lightweight Frisbee. When hit, the two players exchange places. With small groups (about 10) one Frisbee is enough, but use two or three Frisbees with larger groups for a fast-moving game.

Bob Stover

POPSICLE-STICK FRISBEE

The more players, the better for this game—plus you'll need lots of Popsicle sticks (for just 20 players, you'll need a total of 240 sticks). Mark off a fairly large room or a gym similar to a soccer field (see illustration)—two halves separated by a center line, and a goal at each end (a goal should comprise about a quarter of a team's half of the floor).

Give every player a dozen Popsicle sticks, then divide them into two teams. When the clock starts—
• The offensive object is for each player to quickly assemble a pair of Popsicle-stick Frisbees, then try to land as many as possible in their opponents' goal.

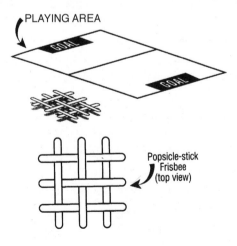

PLAYING AREA

GOAL

GOAL

Popsicle-stick Frisbee (top view)

• The defensive object is to block Popsicle-stick Frisbees from entering their goal.

Rules:
• Players may block flying (or sliding) Popsicle-stick Frisbees any way they wish with their bodies.
• Broken sticks should be removed from the game.
• Players cannot cross the center line or enter their goals.
• Popsicle-stick Frisbees in the goals must stay; but Popsicle-stick Frisbees that land in the playing area may be used again.
• A team may want to designate some players offense, some defense, and some Frisbee builders—or all players can play all positions.

The game continues for a predetermined duration of time, or until all Popsicle-stick Frisbees have landed in a goal. *Len Cuthbert*

ZIMBAT

This game is similar to the game Capture the Flag. Two teams are situated on a large playing field, with a boundary dividing the field in half. Each team is given a flag that they must place in a conspicuous position and protect. Should the other team capture their flag by taking it to the other side, they lose. Players tagged while in enemy territory are captured and sent to jail. The jail is a designated area about 20 yards from the flag zone.

About a fourth of the players are issued Frisbees. Any players tagged by a Frisbee, whether it is thrown or held, are sent to prison, regardless of which side of the field they are on.

Additional rules include the following:
• Jailed players stay in jail for 100 seconds. They count it off themselves and return. There is no freeing of prisoners as in regular Capture the Flag.
• A Frisbee must be dead in order for someone to pick it up. Anyone may pick up a dead Frisbee regardless of who threw it.
• Jailed players must surrender their Frisbees to the nearest person.

Dennis James Henn

GOLF
GAMES

Manicured courses, motorized carts, pitching wedges, polyester pants? Don't need 'em. What you *do* need are people willing to golf with marshmallows, rubber bands, hula hoops, and croquet mallets. For starters. Of course, you'll find lots of variations of regular golf, not to mention several ideas for creating miniature golf courses.

BALLOON GOLF

This game is great in a small game room and can also be played outdoors when there is no wind. First, drop a penny or smooth rock into each round balloon. Then blow the balloon up to about a five- or six-inch diameter. Golf clubs can be made by rolling a full sheet of newspaper into a stick. Cardboard boxes are used as the holes with the par for each hole written on the side of the box. The weight inside the balloon creates a kind of Mexican jumping bean effect causing both difficulty and hilarity for the participants.

• **Balloon Mini-Golf.** Here's another good variation of golf that you can set up in your church.

Provide the kids with plastic floor hockey sticks. These are the golf clubs. The golf balls are small, round balloons (about 4" in diameter). The holes are boxes and containers of various sizes.

Just number all the boxes and containers, and lay out your golf course all over the church—in and out of rooms, down hallways, up stairs, over water hazards (the baptistery), and so on. You might even set up some adverse weather conditions, like placing a fan along one of the fairways. Have someone preshoot the course to establish par for each hole. Since balloons are a bit tough to control, the game can become rather unpredictable, but that adds to the fun. *Wayne Mathias and Mark Boughan*

CROQUET GOLF

This is actually miniature golf played with a croquet set. The wickets are used instead of cups in the ground. Set up your own nine-hole course by arranging the wickets around the yard. Tag each wicket with the hole number as well as placing small signs at each tee where the players must begin each hole. Determine how many strokes will be par for each hole, and indicate this on the tee sign along with the hole number. Try to make each hole different by having to go around objects such as shrubs, through tin cans and tires, and up ramps and hills. Some croquet

sets include wicket tags and tee signs for playing croquet-golf. *Art Volz*

INDOOR PUTT-PUTT

This game is as good as you are creative. If your church has short-pile commercial grade carpet, you have an excellent surface for putting. Design a nine-hole or 18-hole course throughout the building, using obstacles, pews, stairs, or whatever. With masking tape, make each "hole" at least a square foot. (The bigger the hole, the easier it is.) A strip of tape will designate the tee. Use real golf clubs and balls.

Here are a few simple rules:
• The ball must be teed from behind the strip of tape and not outside the length of tape.
• The ball must stop completely inside the taped hole in order to be declared finished. No part of the ball may be touching the tape.
• Balls that rest against or near any object or wall may be placed one club head length from object or wall, but not closer to the hole without penalty.
• Any ball that is unplayable may be moved one club length from where it lies, but not closer to the hole; or it may be returned to the position of the original shot. Players take a penalty of one stroke.

Have scorecards ready for groups of two, three, or four depending on the total number of players involved. If you want to do it up big, have a tournament with a leader board, closest-to-hole contests, and prizes for winners. All ages may play this game, but the younger the ages the more supervision is needed to avoid damage by club or ball. (Excellent game for adults too!) *Thomas Hopewell*

INNER TUBE OPEN

This equalizer can be won by sheer inexperience—so look out, golf pros! You'll need one or two nine-iron golf clubs; a dozen tennis balls (six yellow, six orange); a large blanket, quilt, or tarp; and a large, inflated inner tube.

Mark a line 10 to 12 feet away from the front edge of the blanket; players take their strokes from behind this line. Place the inner tube on the far edge of the blanket.

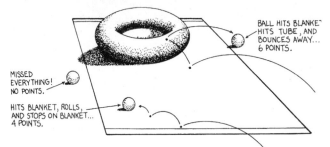

Players get six strokes to earn points in the following ways:

Ball hits blanket	1 point
Ball stays on blanket	3 points
Ball hits inner tube	5 points
Ball stays inside inner tube	20 points

Points are awarded cumulatively. That is, if a ball hits the inner tube (5 points), rolls across the blanket a ways (1 point), and remains on the blanket (3 points), the player earns 9 points. Or if a ball hits the inner tube but bounces away without touching the blanket, that player earns 5 points. Whoever has the most points wins. Play by teams or individually. *Neil Zobel*

KICK GOLF

No green fees for this round of golf. Set up your own nine-hole course: Hula Hoops are the greens, small sticks stuck within them are the flags, and small playground balls are the golf balls. Roll the ball against the stick, and consider it sunk.

For each hole, lay a marker to show where players tee-off. And don't forget to set par: Use hills and other obstacles to vary the difficulty of each hole. Distribute scorecards, and play by teams if you like. *Tammy Larkey and Julie D. Anderson*

LEMON GOLF

Kids get a broom and a lemon. They must hit the lemon with the stick end of the broom onto a piece of paper some distance away. It must stop on the piece of paper. Count the strokes as in regular golf. *Richard Reynolds*

MARSHMALLOW GOLF

This game puts stale marshmallows to good use. Get plastic putting cups from a sporting goods store and a few golf putters. Then lay out a course around the church, using steps, corridors, barriers, and the like. You can even create a few water hazards and traps.

Players may tee up their marshmallow on its side when starting, but once it has been hit, it must be played where and as it is. The marshmallow cannot be rotated or moved to its side, which creates some interesting rolls. It's challenging and fun!

• **Marshmallow Driving Range.** Divide your group in half, into the drivers and the flags.

• **The drivers.** Give all drivers a golf club, a tee, and several marshmallows, then line them up in a straight line about 10 feet apart from each other (enough distance to swing without hitting each other).

• **The flags.** Place the flags at varying distances from the line of drivers. Arm each with three or four marshmallows.

• **The game.** Drivers tee up their marshmallows, aim at the flags, and hit their marshmallows with the clubs. Flags may retaliate by throwing their supplies of marshmallows at the drivers.

• **The point of it all.** The game soon degenerates into an all-out marshmallow war.

• **Marshmallow Wall Golf.** Take your kids on a trip to your homemade driving range. Find a room with a high ceiling and try this low-budget thriller.

The advance preparation is simple. Hang on a wall a large piece of butcher paper that goes from ceiling to floor. Draw a series of greens and a water hazard, each with designated points (see diagram).

Try to hit a marshmallow onto one of the greens with a golf club; if you succeed, you get the number of points marked on the green. If you hit a spot outside of the green, you get the number of points marked in that particular area. If you hit the water hazard, you lose 10,000 points. The person with the highest number of points wins.

Doug Newhouse, Brian Cheek, and Michael Frisbie

RUBBER BAND GOLF

Number nine or 18 paper plates. Tape them onto walls, doors, shelves, lights, or other handy objects, in such a way that they lead from one to the next. These are your golf holes. Using wide masking tape, make a golf tee for each hole and mark it with the corresponding number. Vary the distances from the tee to the hole. The course can include hallways, staircases, and obstructions (like doors), and you can move from room to room or from indoors to outdoors. Be creative!

Use thick rubber bands so teens can write their names on them. Smaller youth groups can have all foursomes start at the first hole, while larger groups might spread out, start at any hole, and play around the course until they have returned to the first hole the team played.

Other options are to include scorecards, establish pars for the course, and set up boundaries. Inevitably, young people will begin shooting one another, but that's half the fun! *Lance Allen*

TENNIS BALL GOLF

Set up a golf course using boxes (big ones for amateurs, small ones for pros) in a park or some other large open area. Golfers toss a tennis ball, attempting to get it inside the box for each hole. Boxes should be numbered one through nine (or 18).

You can make this game as easy or as difficult as you want, depending on the location of the boxes, and how the ball is tossed. You can require that all tosses be underhand, or through the legs, over the shoulder, bounced, or however you wish. Usually a player will put the ball into the box only to watch it bounce out. *Dave Mahoney*

WHIFFLE GOLF

Here's a crazy version of golf that kids will enjoy. Set up your own golf course, anywhere you have room. It can be on an open field, all over a campground, around houses—just about anywhere. Each hole is a small tin can or jar just big enough for a Whiffleball to go into. The cans can be placed on the ground and anchored there, or they can be elevated on poles. After the course is set, each player gets a Whiffleball, and tees-off for hole number one (there can be nine or 18 holes). No clubs are used. You simply toss the ball underhanded. Each toss counts as a stroke. The idea is to get the ball into the can in the fewest strokes possible. In mixed groups the girls can toss overhand, or any way they want. It's best to play in foursomes, just like regular golf, and by setting a par for each hole, printing up scorecards, etc. You can have a Whiffle Golf tournament just like the pros. If you can't get Whiffleballs, you can substitute bean-bags. *Marian Trievel*

Outdoor Games
for Large Groups

These are geared for groups of thirty or more playing in wide-open spaces. No matter how large your group is or what limitations of terrain you face, you'll find contests and activities that will work for you.

AMERICAN EAGLE

This game should be played on grass.

Have players line up next to each other along a line. Their goal is to get across the field to the other line without being tackled by the player in the middle of the field. To tackle properly, the player who is "It" must hold down his prisoner and say "American eagle" three times. The players who make it to the other line must now try to get back to the first line and get past "It" and those who have been tackled. The game continues until everyone has been tackled. Give a prize to whoever lasts the longest. (Place flags in the ground to mark off playing areas if you can't draw lines on the field.)

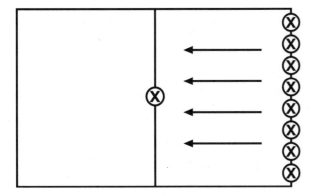

CAPTURE THE FLAG

Set up the playing field like this:

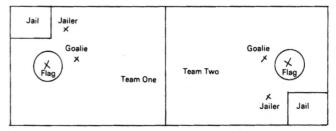

Divide the group into two teams and have them line up on opposite sides of the field. The goal is to capture the opposing team's flag without getting tagged (or tackled or clobbered) by an opposing team player. Players can be tagged only after crossing the center line into enemy territory. After being tagged, players go to jail, which is set up near the enemy team's flag. A teammate can free jailed teammates by tagging them, if he or she isn't tagged before reaching jail. Both get a free walk back to safety.

Each team has a goalie who protects the flag and a jailer who guards the jail. Each team must work out a strategy in order to capture the opposing team's flag.

Furniture Smash

Give each team an old piece of furniture, such as a chair, table, bookshelf, etc., that no one wants back. Each team should also have an 8"x10" piece of plywood with a large hole cut out of its center. The first team to break up its piece of furniture and pass it in pieces through the hole in the plywood wins. Or give each team a small box and a roll of tape. The pieces of broken up furniture must fit inside the box and the box must be sealed up.

Human Lawn Mowers

This game works well in a large yard or park. Give each team one trash bag and every player a pair of blunt children's scissors. Players must cut the grass with the scissors and fill their team's bag with as much grass as possible within five or 10 minutes. No one is allowed to pull the grass by hand. The team with the most grass in the bag wins.

Jousting

This is a great game for camps or outdoor events. Construct jousting poles by using 2x2s about 12 feet long and attaching padding to one end. The padding should be firmly in place and should be soft. Foam rubber covered with towels and plenty of fabric tape has been found to be the best. Two teens challenge each other and each takes a jousting pole. They must stand on a 2x4 on the ground or over a swimming pool and try to knock the other player off with jabs from their poles. They can't swing the pole, only jab with it. *Von Trutschler*

Painters' Caps

Have you tried every possible way to distinguish teams from each other—headbands, arm bands, balloons tied to wrists, etc., etc.? Try dyed painters' caps—you can keep them from event to event or give them to the kids as mementos.

Most paint stores carry inexpensive, cloth painters' caps. Soak them in dye (the Rit brand works well) for 10 to 15 minutes, then tumble dry each color separately. The brighter the colors, the more distinct teams will be from each other when they play games. *Tom Lytle*

Shoe Kick

Have players take off one shoe and hang it off the end of their foot. See who can kick their shoe the farthest. You will be surprised to see how many players wind up kicking shoes over their heads, behind them, or straight up.

Tail Grab

Divide the group into any number of equal chains (a line of people in which each person grips the wrist of the one in front of him). The last person in the chain has a handkerchief tail dangling behind. The object is for each front person to snatch the tail from another line. The fun is trying to maneuver to get someone else's tail while trying to keep your own.

The Blob

Clearly mark off some boundaries, and put spotters on the corners. During the course of the game, anyone who steps outside the boundaries becomes part of the Blob.

One person begins as the Blob. The Blob then tries to tag or chase one of the other players. If another player is tagged or is chased out of bounds, that person becomes part of the Blob. These two join hands and go after a third person who, when tagged, joins hands and helps tag a fourth. The game continues until everyone is part of the Blob. The Blob's only restriction is that it cannot break hands. Consequently, only people on the ends can make legal tags.

For the Blob to be most effective, it must work as a unit. One person should act as the Blob's brain and control the Blob. No tags count if the Blob becomes separated. Once the Blob becomes large enough, it can stretch across the playing field and catch everyone. *Glenn Davis*

TIME WARP TAG

Here's another crazy version of the most famous of all games. You simply play a regular game of tag but at the blow of a whistle, each player (including "It") must slow down to a speed equal to a sports replay "slo-mo." In other words, they must do everything in slow motion. Kids will soon get the hang of it and become very exaggerated in their motions.

Make sure the kids do everything in Time Warp state, even talking and shouting. The game can be played in total Time Warp, or you can blow the whistle for start/stop intervals. Limit the size of the playing area so that several players have a chance to become "It." *Mark A. Simone*

SAMURAI TAG

The only materials needed for this church-wide game are two 3-foot pieces of foam pipe insulation, two Nerf baseballs, and two Nerf bats.

Select two people to be the Samurais. Supply them with the pipe insulation as swords. Anyone the Samurais whack with a sword is frozen in place (à la freeze tag).

Two different people get the Nerf bats. They can unfreeze frozen players with another whack. If players carrying the Nerf bats are whacked by a

Samurai, they are frozen, but they can give the bats to others who can use the bats for unfreezing. One other person must be unfrozen before liberating the person who handed the bat off.

Two other people get the Nerf balls and seek out the Samurais. If a Samurai is hit with a ball, he must trade objects with his attacker (creating a new Samurai). The new ball carrier must count to 10 before moving to allow the new Samurai to get away. If a ball carrier is whacked by a Samurai, he must remain stationary, but he can do what he wants with the ball. The game ends when everyone is thoroughly exhausted! *Jeffrey Crosby*

CROWS AND CRANES

Divide the group into two teams: the Crows and the Cranes. The two teams are lined up facing each other four or five feet apart. The leader flips a coin (heads—Crows, tails—Cranes) and yells out the name of the team that won the toss. If he yells Crows, the Crows must turn around and run, with the Cranes in hot pursuit. If any of the Cranes succeed in touching a member (or members) of the Crows before he crosses a given line (20 to 60 feet away), he is considered a captive of the Cranes and must aid the Cranes when play continues. The team that captures all the members of the other team is the winner. *David Parke*

MARSHMALLOW WAR

Many tag games can be played by using marshmallows as weapons. Kids get three or four marshmallows and may throw them. If they get hit by one, they have been shot. Marshmallows are soft and the white powder on them usually leaves a mark. They may be dipped in flour to make this more so. Wet ones leave a mark also. *Robert Wilson*

MONSTER BUBBLES

Here's a great recipe for giant bubbles that can be used for any number of games and activities. In a large tub mix equal amounts of Joy detergent and water. Add more Joy or water depending on how large you want your bubbles and how soon you want them to pop.

You can make your own personalized bubble hoop by running a string through two plastic drinking straws. Make the hoop as large as you like and then dunk it into the tub of solution. Before you lift the hoop out, put the straws right next to each

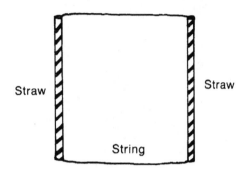

other. As you lift out slowly draw the straws apart. You may have to walk backward to have your bubble form. You can also use a tin can with both ends cut out. Remember, however, that a windy day doth not a bubble make. *Steve Illum*

SARDINES

This game is quite similar to hide-and-seek. The group chooses one person to be "It," who hides while the rest of the group counts to 100 (or until a signal is given). Now the group sets out to find "It." Each person should look individually, but small groups, say of two or three, may look together. When a person finds "It," he or she hides with "It" instead of telling the rest of the group. The hiding place may be changed an unlimited number of times during any game. The last person to find the hidden group, which has now come to resemble a group of sardines, is the loser or "It" for the next game.

• **Wireless Sardines.** This variation of Sardines uses a wireless microphone. "It" takes the microphone and hides within range of the sound system. The rest of the group waits for "It" to give clues about where she's hiding.

If one in the group suspects "Its" location, he tries to track her down. If he fails to find "It," he returns to the sanctuary to wait for another clue. "It" gives a new clue every 30 to 40 seconds. Whoever finds "It" hides with "It" (as in Sardines). The last one to find "It" is the next to hide. *G. Neale Wirtanen and Scott C. McLeod*

TUG-OF-WAR IN THE ROUND

Get a large rope about 24 feet in length and tie (or splice) the two ends together, making one round rope. Four teams line up on the four sides of a large square. In the center of the square, the rope is placed on the ground in the shape of a circle. The teams should be equal in size and each team should number off from one on up. The leader then calls out a number and the four kids (one from each team) with that number grab one side of the rope and try to get back across their team's line. As soon as a player crosses the line (pulling the rope), he is declared the winner. Continue until everyone has had a try. *Roger Disque*

TUG-OF-WAR TIMES TWO

By tying two ropes in the middle so that there are four ends of equal length, you can have a tug-of-war with four teams instead of two. Draw a circle on the ground so that each team is outside the circle when the war begins.

When one team is pulled across the circle line, it is eliminated from the game, leaving the other three teams to tug against each other. Those three play until another is eliminated, and finally two teams play to determine the winner. Each time, the tug-of-war is conducted across the circle.

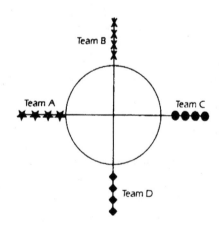

For a Tug-of-War Times Three, just get three ropes and begin with six teams. It works! The primary advantage to this version of tug-of-war is that the least strong teams can gang up on the stronger teams and eliminate them from the game early. *Lew Worthington*

BEDLAM BALL

This is a game that would be good to kick off a camp or retreat, since it can accommodate a few hundred kids divided into four teams. It is really a combination of several games. You play football, soccer, basketball, Frisbee, and giant push ball. The catch is that all four teams must play all five games at the same time, in the same place.

You will need four soccer-type goals. They can be made out of PVC pipe if you want to build your own (see diagram).

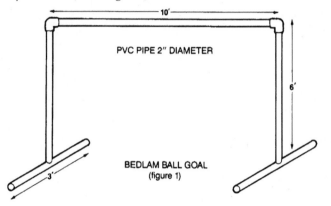

PVC PIPE 2" DIAMETER

10'

6'

3'

BEDLAM BALL GOAL
(figure 1)

Place these goals on the playing field equally distant from the center. With some field chalk, line a defensive zone. This zone is five yards wide on each side of the goal and 10 yards out. In the center of the field, place the giant push ball, 10 footballs, 10 basketballs, 20 Frisbees, and 10 soccer balls. (You could add more or less depending on the size of your group.)

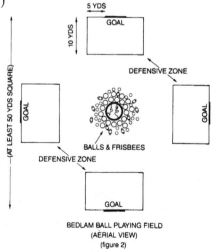

5 YDS

10 YDS

GOAL

DEFENSIVE ZONE

GOAL

GOAL

(AT LEAST 50 YDS SQUARE)

BALLS & FRISBEES

DEFENSIVE ZONE

GOAL

BEDLAM BALL PLAYING FIELD
(AERIAL VIEW)
(figure 2)

The objective of Bedlam Ball is to be the team with the fewest points scored through its own goal. So each team will want to have a defensive unit to guard its goal. Offensively, teams want to

score as many points in the other three goals as possible.

Since the playing area is chaotic, there must be something to designate teams. Try 10-inch balloons and rubber bands. The balloons (each team should have a different color) are distributed before the game begins. Each person has to blow up his balloon, attach the rubber band, and place the balloon on his head so that it stands up straight. (This looks hilarious.) Popping balloons is not allowed. They are for team designation only.

To keep score, place several sponsors at each goal with pad and pencils. They keep up with the points and also watch for infractions of the rules. They are also armed with whistles and flashlights.

The game is played in four quarters of five minutes each. To begin each quarter, the teams gather around their own goal. On the signal they rush out to the balls and begin play. Between quarters the teams regroup, rest, and plan strategy. All the balls are placed back in the center of the field. If played at night, the last quarter can be played with the lights out.

Running is not allowed during lights out. Have two spotlights sweeping the field looking for runners. During the game, play "The Ride of the Valkyries" from *Apocalypse Now* over some very loud speakers. Any wild music would be a good substitute. Additional rules:

• You must keep your balloon on. (Have extras.)
• You may pass or run with the football. The only way to score is to run it through the goal. You get seven points. If you are tackled, you must give up the ball.
• You may dribble or pass the basketball, but you may not run. The only way to score is to throw it through the goal from outside the defensive zone. It scores two points.
• You may only kick the soccer ball. This is the only way to advance or score. Again the scoring kick must come from outside the defensive zone. It scores one point.
• You may pass or run with the Frisbee. You score by throwing it through the goal from outside the defensive zone. It scores one point.
• The push ball can be advanced any way possible. It must go through the goal. It scores 10 points.
• Only your five defensive specialists are allowed to stand in your team's defensive zone.

• Offensively, only someone with a football trying to score, or a group pushing the push ball are allowed in the defensive zone of other teams. All other scoring must be done from outside the defensive zone.

It helps to have an extra-loud sound system to control the game once it starts. Bedlam Ball is fantastically received by teens because it can be fun for the more timid players, yet still have some tough competition for the aggressive kids. *Joey Womble*

BEDLAM BALL
PLAYING OUTFIT
(figure 3)

CANNONBALL RUN

Here is a game which combines creativity with athletic ability. Begin by dividing the group into teams. Each team gets a pile of car parts, one large appliance box, tape, streamers, balloons, markers, tin cans, and anything else they can scrounge up on their own. They have 45 minutes to an hour to build a car.

In the race itself, there are two people per car—a driver and a passenger—who together provide the legpower. There is also one person—the tow truck—who must run alongside the car all the way. If any piece of the car falls off, the tow truck must pick it up, carry it, and—from that point on—must hang onto the shoulder or arm of one of the people in the car.

Every so often in the course—whether it's a long grand-prix-type course or a circular race track—each team must make a pit stop and change crews. It is a good idea to require a boy/girl team in the car each leg of the race. For an added surprise, place an unannounced tollbooth along the way and require exact change to pass. Delay each team one minute for every penny it is short of the seven cents needed to pass. Doorways to buildings and narrow points on the path make great tollbooths.

There are two winners when the race is completed: the team that finishes the course first and the team with the slickest-looking and best-designed car, or what's left of it, when the race is over. *Dan LeRoy*

DRAGON DODGEBALL

Have the entire group form a circle. Pick four to five people for the first team. They are the dragon. These players move into the center of the circle and form a line by holding the waist of the person in front of them. The people who make up the large circle throw the ball at the dragon, trying to hit the last person below the waist. Once hit, the last person returns to the outside circle and players continue to hit the person at the end of the dragon until no one is left. Then a new team goes into the middle. Time each team to see which one can last the longest. *Kathie Taylor*

HILLSIDE HAVOC

If you have a nice open hillside, you might be able to add some new excitement to some of your favorite games like baseball, volleyball, soccer, Capture the Flag, and so on. You can play either up, down, or across the hill, depending on the game. If you're trying to even up two unequal sides in competition, use the hillside to give one side the advantage. If the teams are equally skilled, play games in halves, switching sides in the middle of the game. It really adds a new dimension to game-playing. *Alan Overland*

TUBE MANIA

Here's a physically exhausting game that can be lots of fun. It might be best if played boys against boys and girls against girls.

Mark a large square in the field, and place a stack of seven to 10 inner tubes in the center of the square. Divide the group into four equal teams, each one lining up on its side of the square. Number the players on each team.

The object of the game is to get as many inner tubes as possible across your team's line. Call out several numbers. The players with those numbers run to the center and start dragging the inner tubes to their lines. There may be several players tugging on the same tube. Each tube successfully pulled across a team's line scores one point for that team.

Once the kids get the hang of it, add a soccer ball to the game. Each team gets a point deducted from its score if the ball is kicked over its line. Team members along the team line act as goalies. Once the ball touches the ground behind a team, the point is scored against it.

To further complicate the game, add a cage ball four to eight feet in diameter. The team that gets this ball across its own line gets three additional points. *Rob Yonan*

3-D STRATEGO

Here's a combination of Capture the Flag (see page 49) and the board game Stratego, for which you'll need the standard Capture the Flag equipment—two flags and a big area with plenty of hiding places—as well as a couple decks of playing cards (or Rook cards).

After two teams are formed and they both hide their flags, give each player a playing card—a heart or diamond to Red teammates, and a spade or club to Black teammates. The cards determine a player's rank—the king is the highest; then the queen; on down to the ace, which is lowest. The ace, however, is the only card that can beat a king.

Once play begins, both teams try to capture the opposing team's flag, according to normal Capture the Flag rules. When a tag occurs, both players reveal their cards. The highest-ranking card

wins and continues playing, but the losing player goes to "Central Exchange"—somewhere central in the game—in order to exchange her card for another (of the same color). Only then can that player rejoin the game. If both players in a tag have identical rank, both must go to the Central Exchange and exchange their cards for new ones.

The winner is the first to capture the other's flag and return it to home territory.

For variety, you can make all 10s bombs, which can blow up all other cards. All fives can be members of the bomb squad, who are the only ones able to defeat the 10s. *Rauel Feldheizer*

LIGHTNING STRIKES

For this game you need a dark night, a large open place like a football field or even an empty parking lot, a few old sheets or blankets, and a glow-ball—the kind that glows when you break a cylinder of fluorescent liquid and put it inside the ball. Divide into two teams, assign three to eight kids to a sheet, and align them within their own zones like this on the field:

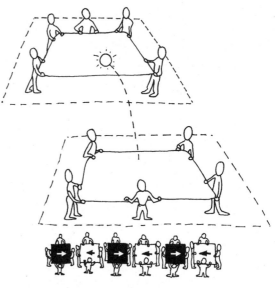

Holding the edges of the sheet and quickly stretching it taut, a team uses it to fling the ball toward the goal at the end of the field. A team gets to fling the ball only when it lands in that team's zone. Goals are at opposite ends of the field, as in football, and each goal earns (why be stingy?—points are free) 10,000 points. Any throwing of the ball by hand, of course, earns 10,000 points for the *other* team.

The visual effect at night is neat—the eerie glow zips and zigs and zags through the darkness. With enough kids, you may want to use more than one ball. *David Washburn*

MISSIONARY

In this game, each team must guide its missionary safely through a field of headhunters (the other team). You'll need to divide into two teams of equal size.

The first team, the missionaries, choose one of their members to travel through a dangerous mission field. That player must put a paper bag over his head and move across the playing field from a starting line to a finish line while trying to avoid being touched by any of the headhunters. Teammates guide the missionary across the field by shouting directions to him, but they must coordinate the directions and shout them in unison to avoid confusion. Teammates cannot walk with the missionary.

Meanwhile, the other team, the headhunters, spreads out over the playing field. They will attempt to impede the progress of the missionary by touching him. They cannot, however, move from their original positions on the field, except once during each round, when they may take three giant steps in any direction. Any contact with the missionary must be made while a headhunter is standing still, so these steps must be planned carefully. The headhunters may also shout false instructions to the missionary, but silence is often a better strategy.

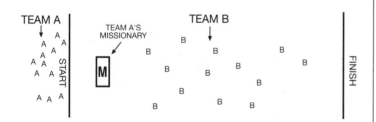

Each team has one chance to guide a missionary and one chance to be headhunters. The missionary is timed from the starting line to the finish line, with a penalty of 20 seconds added for every contact with a headhunter. The team with the lowest time wins. *Ray Wilson*

HUMAN PINBALL

The more the merrier in this fast, fun, indoor or outdoor ball-tag game. Give a playground ball to a group of at least 10, then explain the following rules:

• The object is to be the last one standing. Players who are hit with the ball and fail to catch it must kneel. If someone catches a thrown ball, then the thrower must kneel.

• When players get the ball, they cannot run or walk with it—they must throw from where they obtained the ball.

• Though they cannot move around, kneelers can still play while on their knees. They can stand again if they touch a standing person or hit someone with the ball.

Thud Gudnason

ULTIMATE ELIMINATION

If you have 30 or more kids and a big playing field, this game can continue for a long, exciting time. Students should pair off and tie themselves together at the arm. Throw into the fray several Frisbees, Nerf balls, playground balls, or a combination of them—and it's every pair for itself. When one person of a pair is hit, she can no longer throw, but can only defend her partner. When her partner is hit as well, that pair is out of the game altogether—that is, until the pair that finally eliminated them is itself eliminated. Then the first pair can join the game again.

Just when you think the game is winding down, a lethal pair that eliminated several other pairs is itself eliminated—and competition picks up quickly as those renewed pairs can play again. *Randy Hausler*

A-B-C'S

This game is good for large groups of 40 or more kids. Divide into teams. The leader must locate himself high above the kids, up on a roof, mountain, or other high place, so that he can see all the kids below. He then yells out a letter of the alphabet, and each team must form that letter on the field below as quickly as possible (like a marching band would do). The first team to form the letter wins. Teams may also be judged for the best job of forming the letter in case of ties.

CRAZY KICKBALL

Team One lines up in single file. The first in line is the kicker. Team Two scatters around the field. As soon as the kickball is booted, someone on Team Two gets the ball and everyone lines up single file behind him. The ball is then passed over their heads (or between their legs) until it reaches the last person. Meanwhile the kicker on Team One runs around his teammates and they count each lap. An out is made when the team in the field passes the ball the entire length of their team before the kicker is able to run a lap around his team. Make it two laps if the teams are having difficulty making an out.

GIANT PUSH BALL

Purchase a giant push ball from a sporting goods stores, supply house, or science supply house. It should measure approximately six feet in diameter and will weigh close to 100 pounds. Normally the ball is covered with canvas, and it's guaranteed for life.

A typical push ball game is as follows: Teams line up on either side of an open field. The ball is placed in the middle. At a signal, the two teams try to push the ball through the goalmarkers (flags) that are laid out at opposite ends of the field.

Four teams can play at once. Just have goals on all four sides of the field. The goal can be the entire length of the side of the field if you like.

OUTDOOR GAMES

FOR SMALL GROUPS

Flexibility is the key here. While these games work best
in groups of fewer than 30 people, you can tweak most of them to
work for larger groups, too. And while some require a large playing area,
many can be played in a small yard.

EGGS ON ICE

Hide eggs in the snow (white eggs, of course), give
each team a single flashlight, and send them out to
find the eggs. *Lynne Hartke*

DUMP THE TRUCK

Divide the kids into two teams, and have them line
up facing each other about 15 feet apart. Get two
rubber balls (two- or three-inch diameter). Give one
ball to each team. Then choose two teens, and give
each a toy pickup truck with eggs in the back. Tie a
string so the kids can pull the trucks down the
middle, between the two lines. The two teams then
throw the balls in an effort to break the eggs. If they
tip the truck over without breaking the eggs, they
must wait until it is set up and reloaded with the
dumped eggs before firing again. The two teens
walking down the middle (one behind the other)
walk slowly but may vary the speed somewhat. The
sponsors may vary the walking speed or the distance
apart the teams are as necessary. By crossfiring, the
balls can be kept in quite steady action. Points
should be awarded as follows: One point for every

egg a team breaks, and give the kids pulling the
trucks two points for every egg they bring through
unbroken. Give a prize to the winner. *Robert Vogel*

SCAT

Here's an old game that may be new for your kids.
Everyone is assigned a number. Two numbers are not
assigned to anyone and remain a mystery. The
person who has the ball throws it up in the air and
calls a number. Everyone scatters except the person
whose number was called. He immediately retrieves
the ball and yells "Stop!" He then tries to hit
someone with the ball. If that person is hit, he gets a
letter (S, C, A, or T), and if the thrower misses,
then he gets a letter. Also, if the mystery number
(chosen by the leader) is called, then everyone gets
a letter. People who get four letters, S-C-A-T, are
eliminated. *Glen Richardson*

BALLOON KITE WAR

Here's a great idea for a sunny afternoon at the park,
church picnic, or part of a larger special event. Ask
your kids to bring a kite and a needle to a

predetermined area. Supply masking tape. Don't tell them what is going to happen. Make sure the place you meet is a large open area.

Attach several large weather balloons or large regular balloons filled with helium to strong cords. Have students attach the needle securely to the kite and launch it. The first person to pop a balloon in the air wins. *Dick Baugh*

CLOTHES ENCOUNTERS

You can spend a whole evening making your own UFOs and launching them. This activity is a lot of fun. Be sure to do it in an open area in the winter or where there is no danger of starting a fire. Here's how it works: These UFOs are basically hot-air balloons made out of dry-cleaning bags (usually available for a few cents each at any dry cleaners), a few birthday candles, four plastic straws, and some scotch tape. Insert one end of the first straw into the end of the second straw. Then insert one end of the third straw into the end of the fourth straw. This gives you two double length straws. With a bit of tape, fasten the middles of the two double length straws together to form an X. With scissors or a razor blade, make a three-inch slit along the top of each of the four straws, midway from either end.

In the slits, set four birthday candles (small ones are best). Then while someone else holds the dry cleaning bag open end down, poke the straws through the sides of the bag and secure them with a bit of tape. The candles should be standing up vertically inside the bag. While a couple of people hold the bag up and keep it from collapsing into the candles, light all the candles. In a few seconds, the bag will slowly fill with hot air and rise into the sky. It really is an effective sight. *Marshall Shelley*

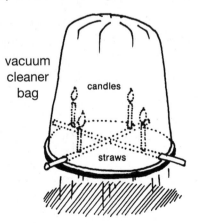

vacuum cleaner bag

candles

straws

HORSEY BACK TAG

This is a wild game that should be played on a grassy area. Each team is made up of a horse and rider. The rider mounts the horse standing on two feet by jumping on the back of the horse with arms around the horse's neck. Each rider has a piece of masking tape placed on their back by the leader so that it is easily seen and reached. When the signal "mount up" is given, the riders mount their horses and attempt to round up the tape on the other riders' backs. The last rider left with tape on her back wins. Only the riders may take the tape off other riders; the horses are just horses. If a horse falls, then that horse and rider are out of the game. *Carl Campbell*

FLOUR OF POWER

Quite a number of games can be created by using two common and easily available items: knee-high stockings and regular all-purpose flour. Place about $3/4$ cup of flour in the toe of the stocking (all sheer works best) and tie the end. The stocking can now be swung, thrown, or slingshotted with a resultant patch of flour being deposited on the surface of whatever it hits. Any tag game can be played with this device (regular tag, team tag, freeze tag, etc.)

One good game to try is to line everybody up on one side of a field with one person in the middle of the field armed with the stocking. At the whistle all must run to the other side without being hit by the stocking. Everyone hit is eliminated. For large groups use more than one person in the center.

These can be used in place of water balloons and they can be used over and over. One filling of flour will last for quite a while. By using your imagination this simple device will bring hours of enjoyment for youths. *Greg Thomas*

HAT AND GO SEEK

Here's a game that combines the best of tag and hide-and-seek. One person wears an old hat, hides his eyes, and gives the rest of the group one minute to run and hide. Then, the hat-wearer begins to search. (The hat must be worn, not carried.)

When someone is found and tagged, that person must wear the hat, cover his eyes for 20 counts, and continue the search. Each person should keep track of how many times he wears the hat. The one who wears it the least number of times wins.

Rusty Zeigler

HULA HOOP HIDE-AND-SEEK

To make a game of hide-and-seek more memorable, provide your youths with Hula Hoops to wear. The Hula Hoops rattle and limit hiding spots. Hula Hoop Hide-and-Seek equalizes the fast and slow runners. *Keith Curran*

HUMAN CROQUET

This game is played a lot like the regular version of croquet, only you use people instead of a croquet set. Set up five or nine people as the croquet wickets who stand in position according to the diagram below with their legs apart.

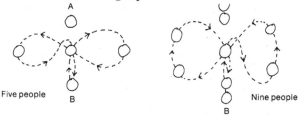

Five people   Nine people

Line up everyone else into two teams, behind the ends (points A and B). The object is to crawl through all the markers (between their legs) on your hands and knees and back to the beginning in a relay race. Each person does it one at a time until everyone on the team has gone. The first team to finish is the winner. *Derek McAleer*

KICK THE CANS

Six empty soft drink cans, the dark cover of night, lots of places to hide, and a large area to play are the only requirements for a game that could last for hours. The hardest part is usually selecting the first person to be "It."

The six cans (it's a good idea to have extras in case these get lost or bent) are stacked three on the bottom, two on the next row, and one on top. Someone kicks the cans to start the game, and while "It" is retrieving and restacking the cans, everyone else hides.

The object of the game is simple: Try to sneak up and kick the cans before "It" can call your name. "It" cannot just stand by the cans, but should look around for people hiding. "It" can go anywhere and can call a person's name at any time he sees them (as long as the cans are stacked). If everyone is called, then the last person caught becomes "It." If someone kicks the cans, though, everybody previously caught is set free. It might be advisable to limit the number of kicks on any one person or else someone may be "It" all night. For example, if a person fails to catch everyone before the kicks or 15 minutes, someone else must volunteer to be "It," preferably someone who has not yet served. Groups of 10 to 12 kids rarely run into this difficulty, however. It is obviously more difficult to catch everyone with larger groups. *Randy White*

RING AROUND THE RIND

This is a great idea for a picnic or day at the park activity. Slice a watermelon like a loaf of bread and pass out the circular sections to each member of the group. Explain that each person must eat their piece without their hands touching anything but the rind and without breaking the slice. When finished, only a green ring of rind should remain. The object is to be the first person to finish eating the inside of the circle. You can offer a prize for the winner—a towel for their dripping chin. *Marshall Shelley*

WALKY TALKY

This is a good game for use on long walks. Have players pair up and walk side by side in a long line. The pair at the front of the line (Pair 1) can go to any other pair in the line (Pair 2 for our purposes) and say "Move forward five pairs." (They choose either direction and any logical number.) Pair 2 moves to its new position and Pair 1 replaces them in their old spot. Follow this same system throughout the game until you get to your destination. If you have a large crowd, you might have two or three couples lead off. This creates a lot of confusion with people running back and forth, but that's the fun of it. *Jan Schaible*

CROQUET POOL

Mark off a 30-by-20-foot area of smooth ground with rope—this is your pool table. For pockets, lay speed cones, small buckets, etc., on their sides at the

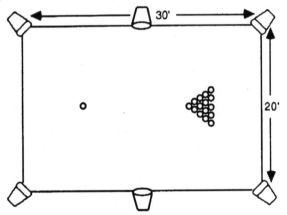

corners and at the midpoint of the 30-foot sides, pool-table fashion. With enough croquet balls for your group (pool uses 15), designate one as the cue ball and begin the game by breaking the triangle.

From here, the game is played just like pool: The first one (or team) to sink his croquet balls into the cones wins. Mark the balls by color, stripe, etc. And don't forget to save the eight-ball for last!
Michael W. Capps

POWER CROQUET

For this croquet variation, the bigger and more rugged the yard (or lot or field) the better. Unlike its traditional, genteel cousin, Power Croquet is set up

with as many obstacles as you can find—or fabricate. For example, set wickets—
- On the bank of a ditch.
- Underneath a parked car.
- So that players must bank their balls off a cement block or a wall.
- So that players must navigate fallen branches.

In short, design a course similar in shape to normal croquet, but one full of obstacles to get over, under, around, or through. Put the ends of the course as far from each other as possible; if you're confined to a suburban lot, at least run the course around the house through both the front and back yards. *Dale Shackley*

MATTRESS STUFF

This game requires the use of those thin, lumpy mattresses that are common at most camps. You will also need to cut a hole in a sheet of plywood the size of a basketball hoop. Or you can use a basketball hoop.

The hole should be about hip high. Two people have to stuff the mattress through the hole without the use of their hands or arms. It takes team work and some hilarious wiggles. If used with teams, use several mattresses (and holes) at once and compete relay-style. *Dave Gilliam*

SCARECROW STUFF

This game works great where plenty of hay or straw is available. Divide the kids into two teams or more depending on the size of the group. Teams have equal-size piles of hay before them. Each team will choose a person to serve as the team's scarecrow. The scarecrows are to stand the same distance away wearing oversized overalls. The object is for each team to use up all the hay in stuffing its scarecrow.

For added laughs have the scarecrows finish the race by running to a certain finish line. *Donald Thorington*

TURKEY SHOOT

This is a fun little game that you can play next time you take your youth group to an amusement park or to the zoo or to any other place where they divide up into small groups and head out on their own. Give each group about 10 chips or tokens (anything will do) to start with. Then, whenever one group spots another in the park, they yell, "Freeze, you turkey!" at the other group. The spotted group must then surrender one chip to the team that spotted them. At the end of the day, the group that comes back with the most chips wins a prize, or gets the best seats on the bus ride home, or whatever. It's a lot of fun, and it keeps the students looking out for each other all day. *Rob Moritz*

INLAND SURFING

Who needs a beach for a beach party? Your kids can surf your backyard turf with this board, made from an old ironing board reinforced with 2x4-foot crossbars that are grooved in order for the board to sit on ropes slung between trees (see diagram). Decorate the top of the surfboard with contact paper

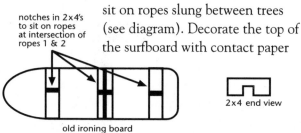

notches in 2x4's to sit on ropes at intersection of ropes 1 & 2

old ironing board (view of bottom)

2x4 end view

and automotive striping, supply a mattress or other cushioning for the inevitable wipeouts, then-watch out! Surf's up as two people shake the ropes to create waves and surfers try their best to ride them out. Run a timed competition—record contestants' best times or the average of several tries. *Jim Bell*

WATERMELON-EATING CONTEST

This watermelon-eating contest is a challenge to eat the most (rather than the fastest). You will need watermelons, one or more scales that measure in ounces, one large bowl for each contestant, and record keepers.

Slice up watermelon, weigh each piece, and insert little flags (made of toothpicks and Post-it notes) indicating the weight. This can be a continuous process as the contest goes on.

Divide your group into teams, or have several players participate individually. Each contestant should have a bowl underneath them to catch water and seeds. Limit the contest to three minutes or less.

As contestants take each slice, the total weight of the piece is recorded. When the watermelon is eaten, the weight of the rind should be recorded also. At the end of the time limit, the leftover seeds and juice collected in the bowls are weighed as well. Add up the weights of all the pieces each player has eaten and deduct the weights of uneaten seeds, juice, and rinds. The total is the player's or team's score. The contestant or team that consumed the most watermelon wins. *Len Cuthbert*

ULTIMATE INNER TUBE

Play this game when you want to put the calculus students in your group on the same competitive footing as the jocks. All you need is an inflated (or partially inflated) inner tube and a large playing area marked with goals at each end.

A team scores by moving the inner tube across the goal line. (You can fling a Frisbee far down field, but an inner tube is a different matter!) Play is similar to football, except that players can run only three steps with the inner tube before throwing it to a teammate. The defense attempts to knock it down or catch it, both of which result in a turnover of control. *Joseph Pent II*

TIRE BOWLING

Just about any service station or tire store will gladly give you some old tire casings (get a variety of sizes and let the kids choose their own). Use either 12 or 20 kids total per setup. Divide them in half and while one group bowls the other acts as the pins. Bowlers should be a set distance from the pins, say 30-40 feet.

The people pins should be set up just like regular tenpins (or six) spaced about two to three feet from each other. The pins are allowed to try to avoid the tire as it comes at them but they must keep both feet planted. If they move either foot at all, the bowler gets the pin. It is best to mark the spot where the pins should stand with a small object like a rock.

Let half the team bowl each time, then switch teams. Next time up let the other half of each team have their turn.

Scoring can be either straight number of pins hit or strikes (three touched with first roll) and spares (three touched with two rolls). If the latter scoring is used, have each pin hit equal three pins, so if two are hit it gives a score of six.

The trick to hitting as many as possible is to wobble the tire and try to get it to fall down in the midst of the pins, striking several as it falls. Casings are dirty, so wear grubbies and have wash-up facilities handy. *Dave Bransby*

GIANT PINBALL MACHINE

Here's an outdoor game that is best played on a grassy slope. At the bottom of the slope, place a few large inner tubes or tires. Stake them to the ground, if possible, and assign each of them a point value. You will also need one or more large, round balls.

Players stand at the top of the slope. Each player aims the ball and gives it a push to roll in the direction of the inner tubes or tires. Points are awarded for each tube or tire that it hits before coming to rest at the bottom. The player must follow the ball to the bottom of the hill without touching it and return the ball to the top.

You can make this even more like a pinball machine by creating teams. When each player takes a turn, fellow team members stand among the tubes in various places. If the ball comes close enough to them (they must remain in the same place), they can kick the ball to score more points (like the flippers on a pinball machine). Try it sometime.

Ronald Allchin

CREATE A GAME NIGHT

The creativity for this game comes from the youths. You supply the following basic materials:
• 4 tennis balls
• 2 garbage cans
• 2 soccer balls
• 2 straws
• 2 cups filled with water
• 2 brooms

Divide the kids into two teams, then give each team their half of the materials. Give them five minutes to make up a game using all the items in a way that everyone will be able to participate. After they have made up the rules, each team takes a turn teaching the other group the game.

As a variation, put three dissimilar items into each of several paper bags—socks, a ball, and a jar; a bucket, a ball, and a stick; paper clips, a bowl, and cotton balls; etc. Then after dividing your group into teams, give each team one of the bags and five minutes to invent a game that uses all three items—and the bag if you want.

Your kids will love the process as much as the games. In fact, Create-a-Game Night might be a hit they'll ask for many times. *Brian Schulenburg and Valerie Stoop*

CRACK THE SAFE

On a safe or trunk is a locked padlock—the kind with 39 numbers on it. The object is to crack the combination and get the prize in the safe—a discount coupon to your next retreat, a free teen devotional book, tickets to a concert, etc.

To find the combination, students comb the building or playing field for the number of objects listed on the sheet—then eliminate those numbers.

To eliminate the last few numbers—or to use by itself to crack the padlock combination—use the maze. (See the sample.) *John McLendon*

JELL-O WRESTLING

Sticky, ugly, disgusting, and terrific fun—everybody brings a box or two of Jell-O, and it's mixed up in a six-foot plastic kiddie pool. Then it's two-minute challenge matches, guys with guys and girls with girls. Have a hose nearby for cleanup. *Dick Read*

SHEET FLING

This game can foster teamwork in your group. You'll need two bed sheets for each team of four people, and big chunks of Jell-O.

Split the foursome into two pairs, then give each pair a sheet that they fold into a 2 x 6-foot rectangle and hold at the corners on the short side. Have the pairs stand side-by-side, two feet apart, and put the Jell-O in the center of one team's sheet. Each team attempts to toss the Jell-O onto the other team's sheet by dropping the center of the sheet and then snapping back the ends so the Jell-O goes flying.

If you want, you can make Sheet Fling mildly competitive by seeing which teams can catch the Jell-O at the greatest distance. Or put Jell-O onto both sheets, and challenge pairs to coordinate a Jell-O swap. *Len Cuthbert*

CRACK THE SAFE!

Instructions: To discover the combination to the padlock, eliminate incorrect numbers by answering each clue listed below, and then crossing off that number from the list below. The numbers left over will open the combination (but you'll still have to figure out the order.)

1 2 3 4 5 6 7 8 9 10 11 12 13 14 16 17 18 19 20 21 22 23 24 25 26 27 28 29 30 31 32 33 34 35 36 37 38 39

Number of large letters on church sign by the road.
Number of outside drinking fountains at church.
Number of french doors into old ambassadors classroom.
Number of letters on the left side of the church bus.
Number of handicapped parking spots.
Number of steps leading into sanctuary.
Number of trophies in sports case.
Number of ceiling lights over basketball court.
Number of chapters in Matthew's Gospel.
Number of days in February 1993.
The last year a person spends as a teenager.
Thanksgiving Day 1992.
Good Friday 1993.
Christmas Day 1995.

So you still have some numbers to cross off? Okay—trace three digits down to their proper combinations, then cross 'em off the above list of numbers.

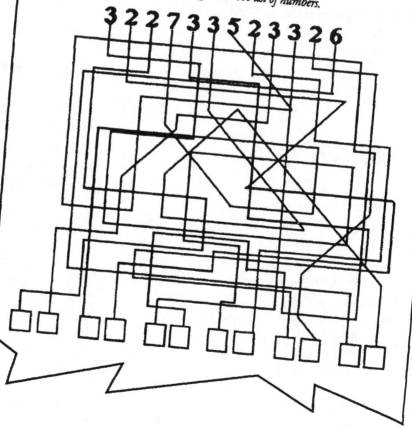

3 2 2 7 3 3 5 2 3 3 2 6

MOUNTED MEDIC SNOWBALL WAR

Here's a new version of one of the oldest games in existence—the old fashioned snowball fight. Divide the group into two teams and play by the following rules:

• Anyone hitting an opponent on the head is automatically out, even if it was done by accident.

• If hit by a snowball, a soldier must fall to the ground and remain there until her mounted medic comes and heals her.

• Each team is allowed one mounted medic. This person must be a gal. Her horse must be a guy.

• The mounted medic must stay on her horse at all times. She may get off only when she must heal a soldier. She heals a guy by kissing him on the forehead. A gal is healed by being kissed by the medic's horse. (Kissing may be replaced by wrapping the wounded part with toilet paper.)

• Players may only be healed by your their mounted medic.

• Anyone hitting either a medic or her horse is automatically out, even if it was done accidentally.

• Each team chooses one king.

• The war is won by assassinating the opposing king, that is, by hitting him on the body, not limbs or head. If the king is hit on the limbs, he must fall to the ground and be healed by the mounted medic. The king may be assassinated while wounded. Anyone hitting the king on the head is automatically out, even if it was done accidentally.

Ron White

SNOW SCULPTURING

This game is great whenever snow is on the ground. Teams of players claim an area of deep snow and sculpt anything they want within the time limit. Encourage them to be as creative as possible. Traditional snowmen are not allowed. Sculptures might include cars, celebrities, buildings, cartoon characters, animals, Santa and his reindeer, etc. Award prizes to sculptures judged the most creative, the most difficult, etc.

STEAL THE BACON

This is a good game for camps or outdoor events and is best with junior highers. Divide the group into two teams, each lined up behind its goal line 20 to 30 feet apart. A handkerchief is placed at a point halfway between the goal lines. Number off the players (the teams are numbered from opposite ends).

The leader calls out a number. The two players who have that number run to the center and try to snatch the handkerchief. Whoever grabs it tries to run back to her own goal without being tagged by the other player. If the hankie-holder gets back without being tagged, her team gets a point. If the pursue tags the hankie-holder, the other team gets a point.

The more skilled players will run into the center and hover over the handkerchief until such a time when he can snatch it and run when his opponent is off guard.

After each successful tag or score, the handkerchief is returned to the center and another number is called. Play for a designated number of points. The leader calls numbers in a manner to create suspense. Include all numbers, and repeat a number now and then to keep all players alert. Also, maintain interest by calling two or more numbers simultaneously, thereby involving four or more players.

• **Stilts Steal the Bacon.** This game works best with four teams. Have the teams line up forming a square (each team on one side of the square). The teams need to be numbered from one to however many are on each team (equal number on each team). A pair of stilts is given to each team and placed about six feet out from each team in the center. A volleyball will make the best "bacon" and should be placed in the middle. When the leader calls a number, those with that number from each team run to the stilts, mount them, and try to go after the "bacon" on stilts and also try to get the bacon back across their side. The team with the highest score wins.

• **Steal the Bacon in-the-Round.** In this variation, draw a large circle (approximately 15 feet in diameter) with lines for line-up which are separate from the circle. By curving the line-up line, all the kids can see the activity without interfering with the action of the game.

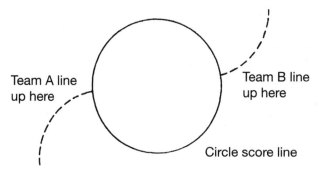

Team A line up here

Team B line up here

Circle score line

Place the "bacon" in the center. The players line up. On the blow of a whistle, the first person on each team, runs to the center and takes the bacon over the circle line at any point. If the person possessing the bacon is tagged, then the tagging person receives the point. If, after a predetermined time (say, 30 seconds) no one picks up the bacon, blow the whistle and the next two players may join the two in the circle. When two team members are working together, they may pass the bacon between themselves.

The advantages of this variation:
• The circle allows for a person to run in any direction to score.
• The teams do not have to be equal; in fact, it is better if they are not equal, so that the players never compete against the same person on future turns.
• You do not have to number off players or call out numbers.
• The game handles large numbers of players and all get a turn.
• **Blanket Pull.** A blanket is placed in the center. A number is called and the two people on each team with that number run out and try to pull the blanket over their own goal line. *Glen Richardson*
• **Blindman Bacon.** This variation of Steal the Bacon works best when played in a circle. Two teams of equal size number off so that there is a player on each team for each number. When a number is called, the corresponding player for each team puts on a blindfold. After hearing the whistle, both players proceed to the middle of the circle, and

with the guidance of screams from teammates, they both try to locate a squirt gun lying in the middle of the circle. Once the squirt gun is found by a player, she then tries to squirt the defenseless player before he can escape out of the circle, behind his teammates. If the player with the squirt gun successfully shoots the other player, a point is awarded to her team. If the other player escapes, his team is awarded the point. The game is made more exciting if, after the blindfolds go on, the leader moves the squirt gun, making it more difficult to locate. *Roger Disque, Norman Jones, and David Rasmussen*

DAVID AND GOLIATH SLING THROW

Divide the group into two teams, with the same number of guys and gals on each team. Each team is given one old nylon stocking and one Whiffleball to place in the toe of the nylon. One person of the same sex steps forward to the throwing line. Each twirls the nylon with the ball in it over his head or at his side and sees who can throw it the farthest. The winner gets one point for his team. The team with the most points wins the contest.

You can then repeat this contest for accuracy. Set a "Goliath" (a person, chair, or other object) approximately 30 feet away from the throwing line. The person that comes the closest gets one point for her team. If she hits Goliath, an additional bonus point is awarded to the team. The kids will quickly find out that it took a lot of practice for David to become such a skilled marksman.

Be sure that the teams are 10 yards to the sides of the throwing line because the slings can go forward, backward, or straight up with amateurs throwing. *Samuel Hoyt*

PENGUIN GAMES

Give each person a rag about four inches wide and two feet long (old bedsheets torn into strips work well). Players then tie the rags securely around their knees so that running is impossible. Players can move only by shuffling their feet along the floor.

Divide into teams and play football using a Nerf football. The game takes on a hilarious dimension when players must hike, run, throw, and kick with their knees tied together. Of course, this opens up the possibility of playing Penguin Baseball, Penguin Volleyball, Penguin Soccer, and countless other games! *Susan DeWyngaert*

JUMPING CATAPULT

This game could be set up permanently outside and could become a year-round challenge whenever things get boring. Set up a catapult (see diagram)

with a ring drawn on the ground a few feet away. Using a playground ball, the kids then try to catapult the ball to the center of the ring. The closest one wins. *Paul Warder*

PILLOW DUELING

Divide into two teams, lining players up parallel but facing away from each other. Number off the kids on one team; then, starting at the opposite end, number off the kids on the other team.

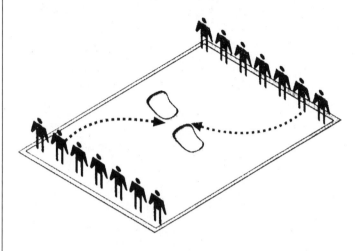

Place two pillows between the teams. Call a number. The players with the number grab a pillow and duel until one has wacked the other five times or until you blow a whistle. Give a point to the team whose player dominated.

You can vary this game by letting the kids line up in any numerical order they wish—or by adding more pillows and calling more numbers.

Jim Ramos

RELAYS
AND RACES

RELAYS AND RACES

Nothing fosters a sense of teamwork, camaraderie,
and often pandemonium quite like a good old relay race. Relays require
team members to perform a given task, one teammate after another, as quickly
as possible. Relays call for teams of equal numbers and can be run indoors
or outdoors with nearly any size group.

BEAT THE CLOCK

Face it—it's probably funnier watching your friends
in a crazy relay race than racing yourself. So for a
change of pace, try running your favorite relay races
not directly team against team, but one team at a
time—against the clock. And enjoy the laughs!

Marti Lambert

BUMP RELAY

Teams of 10 or so are seated in chairs lined up relay
fashion. At a given signal, the first one in line leaves
his seat and rushes to the back of his line, then—

with some adept hip
action—bumps the
teammate off his chair
to the right (see
diagram). The bumped
one moves forward a
chair and bumps that teammate off to the left—and
on to the front person, who runs around to the rear
of the line and starts the process over again.

First team to return to its original chairs wins.

James C. Lutes

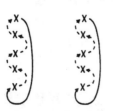

CHEWING GUM RELAY

This is a relay race for two or more teams using
sticks of chewing gum, work gloves, and shopping
bags. Individual sticks of gum (wrapped) are placed
inside the shopping bags, and each team is given a
pair of work gloves. Players put on the gloves, run
down to the bag, pull out a piece of gum, unwrap it
and chew it (with the gloves on), run back, and
then pass the gloves to the next person. The team
that finishes first is the winner. *Jeffrey Collins*

THE DOUGH-TONGUE SHUFFLE

This is a relay game in which the young people are
divided into two equal groups. Each group lines up,
with players one behind the other. Then the first
person in each line is given a large donut (preferably
plain). On a signal, the first person in each group
must run up to and around a given obstacle while
holding the donut by sticking his tongue through its
hole—no hands allowed. (This usually requires that
the head be tilted back and the tongue pointed
upward.

After running around the obstacle, he must go to a designated area where a judge is waiting. Then each runner must eat his donut (to the satisfaction of the judge) and receives another donut from the judge (in his hand). The runner then carries this second donut to the next person in the relay line. The first runner places the donut in position on the next runner's tongue, and the relay continues. The first team to complete the relay by running all its members shouts "THE DOUGH-TONGUE SHUFFLE!" and wins.

Joe Harvey

SHOVEL TROUBLE

Shovel in hand, the first player on each team skateboards to a common pile of spuds at the other end of the lot, shovels up one potato, skates back to his team, deposits the potato in his team's box or basket, then passes both shovel and skateboard to the next teammate, who follows suit.

NOSE KNOCKERS

Ever watch a game end in chaos as students who were supposed to move an object using their noses began to use anything they could to win? Nose Knockers are simply nose extensions that will restrain cheating by making the games easier to perform while providing some great camera shots.

Purchase some paper cups and poke a hole on two sides of the cups. Attach a large rubber band to the holes to allow students to place the cups over their noses like masks (see diagram). Use nose knockers in relay games with golf balls, Ping-Pong balls—even dead roaches. *Rob Marin*

The game continues as long as the taters last; when they're gone, teams count what they've collected. The team with the most wins. Long-handled shovels work better than those with short handles—but the short-handled ones are more of a challenge to work with. *Michael W. Capps*

BEEF JERKY CHEW

Place a package of beef jerky on a table 10 feet in front of three volunteers. On a signal the volunteers race to the table, grab a piece of jerky, and eat it as quickly as possible. The one whose mouth is completely empty first is the winner. *Amy Zuberbuhler*

CAKE RELAY

Each teammate runs a different leg in this relay, passing not a baton from runner to runner, but a cake (store-bought pound cake on a paper plate, or even Twinkies, melons, etc.).

The first leg could be an obstacle course of any kind; the second, a walking race (those who run are penalized by having to stand for 15 seconds); the third, a swim across the pool or waterfront in such a way that the cake stays above water; the fourth leg could require the runner to be blindfolded and directed verbally by a partner; the fifth, an all-out sprint for a quarter-mile or so.

After the last teammate crosses the finish line, the teams must eat the cake before the race is over. After all the wear and tear the cakes have endured—dropped, soaked, manhandled—this climax is hilarious. This game is a great group builder that requires teamwork, and it can be adapted to any situation. *Jon Davis*

WHISPER THE FLAVOR RELAY

Using assorted flavors of Lifesavers or other hard candy or jelly beans, play this relay in which team members guess the flavor of the candy they are tasting.

Divide the group into teams of five to eight players. Each team chooses one member to be the distributor, to whom you give plastic sandwich bags of candies that are identified by flavor. The teams line up in columns, with their distributors standing about 10 feet away from the head of the line. On the signal the runner races to the team's distributor, receives a piece of candy, and races back to the team. The runner puts the candy in the mouth of the second person in line (the eater), who should not see the color of the candy. As soon as the eater recognizes the flavor, she whispers the name of the flavor to the runner, who returns to the distributor and whispers the flavor the eater guessed.

If the guess is correct, the runner races to the end of the line, and the eater then becomes the new runner. Play continues as before.

If the eater's guess is incorrect, the runner returns to the eater to ask for another guess, then returns to the distributor to repeat the guess in a whisper. (If all distributors give out the same flavors of candy at the same time, one team could hear the guess of another team if the guessing is not done in whispers.) Repeat this process until the correct flavor is guessed.

The team that is first to return its initial runner to the front of the line is the winner. *Greg Miller*

FOOD TRANSPORT RELAYS

Both of these relay races involve carrying food from a nearby table, sitting next to each team line, to a far one—all without using one's hands. The results are delightfully messy.

• **Flour Dripping.** On each team's near table is a large bowl filled with flour. On the far table is a similar, though empty, bowl. Each player receives a six-ounce Styrofoam cup.

One at a time, holding the cup with teeth only (no hands allowed), a student fills the cup with flour. Then she runs across the room to the other table, and—still using no hands—dumps as much flour as possible into the empty bowl there.

When all players have run once, the team that transferred the most flour wins.

• **Puffed Rice Relay.** On each nearby table is a bowl of water or milk and a bowl of puffed rice

TEAMING UP

The challenge that every leader faces when it comes to game time is how to divide the group into teams so that the competition will be relatively even. The old "one-two, one-two method" really does not work well because it does not guarantee balanced strenth and the kids can rig the teams by switching places. Or, 15 are on one team and nine are on the other and each vows with gusto that he is on the right team.

What is a leader to do? Back up 10 yards and punt? No! Outsmart those tricky young people.

Have the guys line up according to height and have the girls line up according to height. Simple, right? Now use two different colored felt pens (for example, red and black). Have each guy hold out his right hand, and place a mark (red on one, black on the next) on the back of his hand. Do the same with the girls. If there is switching going on among the guys before you mark them, then mark two in a row red and mark two in a row black. Repeat until all are marked. Then do the same with the girls.

If you prefer not to mark the kids, then number them 1, 2, 3, 4, 1, 2, 3, 4, and so on. Then say the ones and the twos will be on the same team and the threes and the fours will be on the same team. This method will assure the best possible mixing of individuals, an even number of guys and girls on each team, a safeguard against having the teams rigged ahead of time, and an even distribution according to size. *Samuel Hoyt*

cereal. Far tables each have an empty bowl on them.

At the signal, the first player in line dips his face into the water or milk, and then into the bowl of cereal (oatmeal works well, too). The goal is to get as much cereal stuck to his face as possible. As usual, no hands allowed.

Now the player with the puffed-rice face dashes to his team's far table, where he tries to get the cereal off his face and into the bowl—still without hands. When all players are done, the team with the most cereal in the bowl wins. *Bret Luallen*

CHOCOLATE AND GLOVES RELAY

Gather pairs of gloves (rubber gloves and ski gloves work well) and a bag of chocolate miniature candy bars. Put the candy in a big bag. One player from each team runs to the bag, puts gloves on, grabs a piece of chocolate, opens the wrapping, eats the chocolate, and removes the gloves before racing back to tag the next teammate. *Duane Steiner*

SODA SLURP RELAY

This relay generates lots of belches—and is therefore perfect for junior highers. Prepare enough double straws—two straws made into one by inserting the end of one into the other—for everyone to have one. Break out a couple liters of soda, and have a race to see which team can suck the soda out of the container through the double straws the fastest. Here's the catch: The double straws suck up not only soda, but air (through the joint where the straws are connected). The team that finishes its soda first wins.

Let the belching contest begin after the relay.
Duane Steiner

EGG AND ARMPIT RELAY

Divide into teams and place half of each team against opposite walls. One person puts the handle of a spoon into her mouth and a raw egg on the bowl of the spoon. She races to the other side of the room. The receiving teammate puts the egg in his armpit, grabs the spoon, and races back across the room. The next teammate takes the spoon and holds it while the runner drops the egg from his armpit onto the spoon. The race continues back and forth until one team is the first to have all teammates make a successful run.

EGG AND SPOON RELAY

Divide into teams and give each player a spoon. Teammates line up alongside each other. The teammate on the far right has a dozen raw eggs lying on the floor beside him. The first player picks up an egg, puts it on his spoon, and passes it to the next person, who passes it along, using only the spoons. The winning team is the one that gets the most unbroken eggs down the line in the least amount of time.

For variation, use marbles instead of eggs.

GREAT CHICKEN RACE

This is a relay for pairs. The gal jumps on the back of a blindfolded guy and runs him through an obstacle course by giving him directions. To make it a bit more difficult, she is handicapped by having a raw egg in her mouth. If she breaks it, it messes up both of them. *Larry Houseman*

LEMON PASS

In this relay, team members pass a lemon down the line using only their bare feet. They should hold the lemon by cupping it in the arches of their feet while lying on their backs. The first team to pass the lemon all the way down the line wins.

LIFESAVER RELAY

Divide the group into teams (at least seven players each), and have teammates line up alongside each other. Each player is to hold a toothpick in her mouth, using it to pass a Lifesaver candy (with a hole in the middle) along the line. If the candy is dropped, it must be quickly sent back by hand to the beginning of the line and be started down the line again. The winning team is the one whose candy reaches the end of the line first.
• **Spaghetti Relay.** For variation, use uncooked spaghetti instead of Lifesavers and straws instead of toothpicks.

Divide your group into relay teams of any size and give each player a nonbendable drinking straw. Players fold the end of their straws (about an inch from the end, so the spaghetti won't be inhaled or become soggy from saliva) and then grip the straws in their teeth.

Start the relay by placing a whole piece of uncooked spaghetti into the straw of the first person. Without using hands, that person must slide the spaghetti into the next person's straw. The action is repeated until the spaghetti reaches the end of the line. Then, the last person must run to the front of the line as soon as possible.

If a piece of spaghetti drops, the person in the front must start the whole process over again with a new length of spaghetti. *Greg Miller*

GREAT SPAGHETTI RELAY

Divide the group into teams. Each person gets a potato chip (the larger, the better). Each team lines up, and the first person in line holds his potato chip in his mouth. A wet spaghetti noodle is then draped over the chip and the person must run to a set point and back. On returning, he passes the noodle on to the next person, who does the same thing.

The rules:
• No hands are allowed.
• If the noodle drops off, breaks, or becomes mutilated, the player must return to the line, get a new one, and start over.
• If the potato chip breaks or becomes too soggy, the player must get a new chip and start over. The game continues, and the first team to finish is the winner.
Keith Geckeler

PEANUT BUTTER RELAY

Divide the group into teams with an equal number of players on each team. Then have the teams line up single file. A glob of peanut butter (or other such gooey substance) is placed on the person's nose at the end of each line. He then passes the glob to the next person and so on down the line. Prizes are awarded for speed and for the biggest glob on the last person's nose. This game is only for groups with strong stomachs. *Dave Phillips*

ROOT BEER RELAY

Get some cold root beer and at least 10 plastic root beer mugs. Five contestants from one team sit on one side of a picnic table, and five from the other team take the opposite side of the table. Each begins with a full mug of root beer in front of them.

Blow the whistle and the first person on each side starts drinking her root beer. When finished, she sets her empty mug on the table and the person next to her starts to drink, and so on down the line. Meanwhile the ones who have finished are getting refills. When the last person is finished, it starts over again with the first person. It's that second time through that makes this game really wild. The first team to finish the second round wins.

If you have a lot of teams, compete tournament style. *Dan Brandel*

FRUIT BASKET FLY-BY

In this game, each team has two baskets, one filled with fruit at one end of the room, and the other empty at the other end of the room. Teams must compete to see who can be first to get all the fruit from one basket to the other. The trick, however, is that the fruit can only be transported by fruit fly players who fly by having their teammates carry them aloft and over a barrier of chairs or tables across the middle of the room.

Each team divides into halves. Then one-half goes to the side of the room with the full basket and one-half to the side with the empty one. On a signal, one player from each team on the side with the full basket becomes a fly. They must tuck a piece of fruit under their chins, hold their arms out like wings, and be carried by their teammates up to a row of chairs or tables that separate them from the other side. There, the fly is carefully passed to the other half of the team waiting on the far side of the barrier. (After passing the fly over, carriers can crawl under or climb over the barrier to help carry the fly on the other side as well.)

Teammates on the other side then carry the fly to the empty basket, into which he drops the piece of fruit. The fly is let down, and immediately a new fly must be chosen to carry another piece of fruit, and so on until all the fruit has been transported. If necessary, after all the players have served as flies, some can repeat the role. If a piece of fruit is dropped en route, the fly must land, pick it up, tuck it under her chin, and take off again as before. Team to complete the task first is the winner. *Lee Strawhun*

THE GREAT PEW RACE

If your church has bench-type pews in the main building, here's a way to put them to good use.

Divide your group into small teams of three or four kids each. Have them all gather at one end or the other of the church (whichever has the most room). On the signal, the kids all dive under the first pew and crawl all the way to the other end of the church and back under the pews.

The first team to have all its players return is the winner. *Tracey Werner*

INDOOR OBSTACLE COURSE

This relay game is best played by two or more teams. Because of the time necessary to complete the obstacle course, it's best to limit each team to six players or less.

Set up the course as shown in the diagram. Each player is given a soda straw. On the signal, the first player from each team goes to the starting position to pick up one of five kernels of corn from a paper plate. The only way they can move the corn, however, is by sucking on the straw and creating a vacuum that holds the kernel while they walk over to a foam cup on the near side of a table five feet away. Once they reach the cup, they drop the kernel in it and go back for the next one, continuing until all the kernels have been moved. If a corn is

dropped en route, the player picks it up again using the same method and continues.

Once all five kernels are in the cup, players must blow the cup across the table (the wider the table, the better) and make it land in a box placed on the floor underneath the table's far edge. If the cup or any of the corn misses the box, the cup must be refilled by a designated assistant from the player's team and then replaced on the table's edge. The player keeps trying until the cup and corn all fall into the box at once.

Next, players crawl under the table, grab a jump rope on the other side, and jump with it to a spot 20 feet away, where a pile of deflated balloons is waiting. They blow up one balloon until it bursts, then run to a tape mark on the floor five feet away. There they must pick up two plastic rings from the floor and toss them around a small can three feet away. (Empty bread crumb cans work well for this.) When the players have made a successful toss with both rings, they crawl back under the table and tag the next person (and probably collapse). The first team to complete the relay wins.

The game is as much fun to watch as it is to play, so kids who don't want to run the course may enjoy acting as assistants. Besides helping out with unsuccessful cup-blowing attempts, the assistants must also replace the cup on the table and the corn on the plate after the player has succeeded in that part of the relay.

As a variation you can use a stopwatch and allow individual players to compete against the clock. *June L. Becker*

HUMAN OBSTACLE COURSE

For this relay, each team lines up single file behind a starting point. Use 10 additional team members as obstacles: pole to circle around, leg tunnel to go under, kneeler on all fours to leap over, sitter with outstretched legs to step among, etc. At the signal, the first person in line goes completely around the pole, under the tunnel, over the kneeler, among the sitter's legs (not missing any stepping space), finishes maneuvering around any other obstacles and then runs back. The other players take their turns. If an obstacle is missed or improperly executed, the runner must repeat that obstacle. You can also let the obstacles decide how the runners have to get by them. When the first runner approaches, the obstacle says, "Run around me three times," or "Crawl between my legs." Pairs can work together to create obstacles for even more variety.

Norman "Beetle" Bailey and Ruth Staal

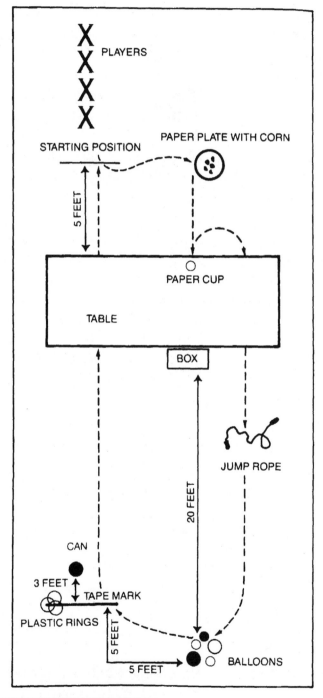

TIRE GRAND PRIX

Lay out a course around the church buildings or down roads that are closed to traffic, and give everyone an old tire. Old tires may be borrowed from a cooperative tire dealer or service station. Have a race rolling the tires around the course. For larger groups, make it a team relay, with kids stationed every 50 yards along the course. The tire is passed on at each "pit stop" to a fresh "driver." The first player (or team) to complete the course wins. For added fun, allow players to kick, knock over, or in any way impede the progress of the opposition's tire. *Gene Poppino, Jr.*

LONG JUMP RELAY

Divide contestants into teams of six or eight, mark a starting line, and have kids stand by teams in single file behind it.

At the signal to go, each leader does a standing broad jump straight ahead (both feet must leave the ground simultaneously). The next in line then runs up to him, places his feet exactly where the leader's feet are, and does another standing broad jump. The third player runs up to the second and repeats the process. Likewise, each player in turn rushes forward and jumps from where the preceding player landed.

After the last player of every team has jumped, the total distance of each team is measured, and the farthest distance wins. *James C. Lutes*

MUMMY RACE

This relay requires teams to wrap up a teammate completely in cloth strips and then carry them up to the line and back. Each teammate is so wrapped and toted. First crypt of mummies finished with this sepulchral task wins. *Tom Jackson*

A DAY IN MY LIFE RELAY

Here's a wild, indoor obstacle course that's won by the team with the lowest combined time. You can run one player at a time, or set up two rooms and run players from opposing teams simultaneously.

You'll need these objects in the room:
• "Bed" with sheet, blanket, and pillow.
• Table with wash basin, towel, comb, bowl, cereal, milk, and spoon.

• A pair of oversized pants, a similarly baggy shirt, a huge pair of shoes, a bulky coat, five to 10 pieces of trash, five or so books, an umbrella, and a pen–all of them strewn over the floor.

A few feet away from the room, set up a class—a table where a "teacher" sits across from whom is an empty chair for the player. The teacher is equipped with a sheet filled with lots of questions of the following sort that he'll orally quiz each student with:

1. Solve this problem: Multiply 12 and 12, then divide that sum by 12, subtract 12 from the remainder, and then add 12 to that. Then give the correct answer to the problem three times four. (Answer: 12)

2. What color is the color blue? (Blue)

3. How do you spell Vinnie Smith's last name? (S-M-I-T-H)

4. If your mother is twice your age, and your father is two times as old as you, and your sister is only half your age, and Calley, your sister, is five— then tell me what your sister's name is. (Calley)

5. What direction would you face if you turned to your right after originally facing south? (West)

Each player begins in bed. All the props are positioned for each player before her turn (trash scattered on floor, cereal bowl and spoon in place, etc.). When the alarm goes off, the timing begins— and the player must race through the following routine (each team may have a coach to make sure players do the right things in the right order):

1. Jump out of bed.
2. Make the bed neatly.
3. Dress for the day.
4. Clean up the trash.
5. Wash face and comb hair.
6. Eat breakfast.
7. Collect books and pen for school.
8. Put on coat.
9. Open umbrella.
10. Run to school and take the test.

When a player scores 100 percent on the test, the clock stops, the time is recorded—and when everyone's had a turn, the team with the lowest total time wins. You may tie this game in with a video visit to the kids' own bedrooms or with a Bible study about peaceful coexistence with parents and house rules. *Mark Ziehr*

PIE TIN TOSS

For this game, you will need to secure the use of six high hurdles, like those used at a track meet. If you can't get real ones, just improvise. Line the hurdles up as in a regular hurdle race.

Team members run with a pie tin filled with shaving cream. When they come to the hurdle, they must throw the pie tin into the air, go under the hurdle, catch the pie tin on the other side, and continue until they have gone under all six hurdles. That person then runs back and tags the next team member in line, who repeats the action.

Each team is timed, and the best time wins. If a runner drops a pie tin, she must go back to the beginning and try again. *Linda Thompson*

SCHOOL CRAZE

This relay race is a back-to-school event. Two teams race each other through a battery of school-like

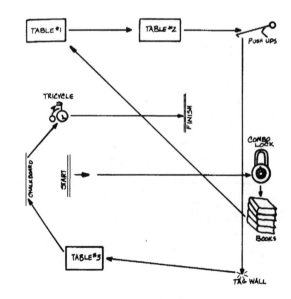

tasks, with each teammate responsible for one leg of the relay. Set up a large room with the necessary equipment and furniture (see diagram).

1. At the sound of the tardy bell, a team's first member sprints across the room, opens a combination lock (the combination is written on a piece of paper taped to the lock), then tags the second member.

2. This teammate picks up a large stack of books (make it challenging, but don't cause any hernias) and, stopping to pick up any that he drops, staggers across to table 1.

3. Once the books are plopped down, the third member may turn over a paper on which is printed a maze.

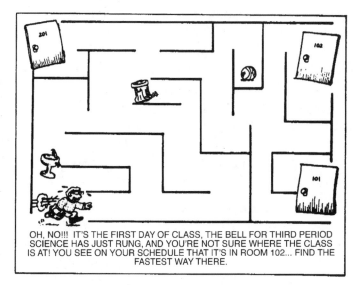

OH, NO!!! IT'S THE FIRST DAY OF CLASS, THE BELL FOR THIRD PERIOD SCIENCE HAS JUST RUNG, AND YOU'RE NOT SURE WHERE THE CLASS IS AT! YOU SEE ON YOUR SCHEDULE THAT IT'S IN ROOM 102... FIND THE FASTEST WAY THERE.

When the maze is completed, the teammate takes the maze to table 2, where a teacher (a sponsor) corrects it.

4. If the maze passes the scrutiny of the grader, the next teammate performs five push-ups, then races to tag the opposite wall before sprinting to table 3. (This is P.E.)

5. Now it's lunchtime. When the sprinter arrives at table 3, the fifth member waiting there must consume a burger and small Coke before dashing to the chalkboard and tagging the sixth teammate.

6. At the board, this member first solves a math problem previously written but covered until now, then copies a short phrase like "More homework" or "Biology's great!" (for composition) before racing to the next and final teammate on a waiting tricycle.

7. Time to go home. When the tricyclist is tagged, he pedals like mad for the finish line across the room.

Roger J. Rome

SHIRT BUTTON RELAY

The object of this relay is (have you guessed yet?) to run up to a shirt and unbutton it. The next player must then rebutton it and so on through the line of players. *Tom Jackson*

BUCKLE UP RELAY

You'll need one bench seat per team for this game (the van variety, with seat belts attached); the removable seats from minivans work fine. Place the bench seats at a starting line. At a designated distance mark a finish line. Divide the kids into two (or more) groups. Place half of each team at the starting line and the other half at the finish line.

Instruct the first three at the starting line on each team to belt themselves into the van seats. On "Go!" the three belted-in players of each team stand to their feet and lumber toward the finish line, lugging the bench seat with them. When they arrive at the far line, they set the seat down, release the seat belts, and the second set of three strap themselves in and race back. Play continues until one team wins by releasing the belts of the final three racing members of the team. *Jerry Meadows*

CENTIPEDE RELAY

Form equal teams of six to eight kids each and line up, alternating boy-girl. Instruct teams to back up to the wall at one end of the room, leaving three to four feet between the last person and the wall.

At the signal each team takes three short steps forward. As soon as the team has moved forward the last step, the first players in the lines break away to the right and run around their team three times as fast as possible, finally taking their place at the back of their team's line. Once in place, the runner yells, "Go!" and the process repeats with three more steps and new front runners. The relay continues until the line itself arrives at the youth leader standing at the other end of the room, or crosses a line on the floor.

The room doesn't need to be large, since teams don't need that much room to move forward. They mainly need room on the sides of the lines to run around their teams without bumping into the competition. For every three steps forward, the team loses one body-space backward since the runner takes his place at the end of the line.

As a true test of speed and skill, each person tries to run around the team faster and faster. The key to winning this relay, however, is for everyone to press as close as possible to the people in front of and behind them. To make each line tighter, instruct players to grasp hold of the waist of the ones standing directly in front of them. (The kids may feel awkward doing this at first, but they'll comply as soon as they see their team losing the race.)

Be sure to point out that each person on the team may have to run several times in order for the entire team to reach the marker at the other end of the room. Also point out that the three short steps must be short. Demonstrate how they can move forward by simply placing one foot directly in front of the other and moving. *Michael W. Capps*

CENTIPEDE RACE

All you need for this game are some benches (without backs). Seat as many youths as possible on each bench, straddling it like a horse. When the race starts, everyone must stand up, bend over, pick up the bench between their legs, and run like a centipede. The finish line should be 40 or 50 feet away. It's a lot of fun to watch. *Alan Overland*

CONNECT FOUR

For this intimate relay either divide a large group into teams of five or six pairs, or ask the entire group to pair up and form a line of pairs. The first pair places a rubber playground ball between them at stomach level. To help keep the ball from falling and to help maintain balance, the two players place their hands on each others' shoulders. At a signal the next pair in line, in the same stance, tries to get the rubber ball from the first pair not with their hands, but by securing the ball between them at the stomach (see diagram). The object is to pass the ball as quickly as possible from one set of people to the next without letting it fall. *Michael W. Capps*

GOLF BALL AND PLUNGER CAP RELAY

Have the camera ready for this game! Make two teams and give a plunger (a plumber's helper) and a golf ball to each team. Ask the first player on each team to unscrew the wooden stick from the plunger and place the golf ball where the stick screwed in.

Players in this relay now must walk a prescribed course with the plunger cap on their heads, and the golf ball balanced on the plunger cap. (The course can be simple—out 10 or 20 feet, around a chair, and back, for example.) Players who drop the ball return to their line and start over. For more of a challenge, place obstacles in the course, make the kids walk it backward, etc. *Rob Marin*

MOMMY CONTEST

Each relay team chooses one member to be the baby, who goes to the far end of the room. Each of the remaining members of the teams have specific responsibilities. Make up some variations of your own if you have more than six players on a team.

All players begin their turns by donning the team's mommy costume and running to the baby.

They end their turns by removing the costume back at their line before passing it on to the next teammate.

• First mommy—diapers the baby with a large sheet.
• Second mommy—seats the baby in a high chair and then feeds the baby a jar of baby food.
• Third mommy—cuddles the baby, feeds it a bottle of milk, and burps it (at least two pats on the back).
• Fourth mommy—sets the baby in her lap and rocks it, singing the designated number of verses of "Old MacDonald Had a Farm" and making appropriate barnyard sounds during the song (moos, clucks, baas, etc.).
• Fifth mommy—the team forms a stroller (two players on hands and knees for wheels, etc.) that mommy pushes to the baby and puts the baby in.

The first team to push the baby across the finish line wins. *Stephen May*

ODDBALL CRAWL

Begin this relay by creating two or more teams of eight to 10 players wearing their grubbies. At one end of a long room, line the teams up alternating boy-girl-boy-girl on each team. In each line players get on their hands and knees side by side on the floor. At the signal, the players at the end of each team's line closest to the wall begin crawling over and under their teammates as fast as possible. The stationary players alternately drop to the floor or arch up their backs (still keeping hands and feet on the floor) to make passage quicker for their traveling team member.

As soon as possible after the first players have crossed the second players, the second players may begin their trip over and under the stationary teammates. When traveling players reach the end of the line, they either lie flat or rise up to allow other players to pass over or under them. The relay continues until everyone on the team has successfully crawled over and under the rest of the team. The team that completes the relay first is the winner.

If your group is too small for two teams, form one team and play several rounds to go for the fastest team time. Have a camera handy to catch some of the action.

Awkward personal contact is rare, for the youths are sufficiently caught up in the race that they don't take time for mischief. *Michael W. Capps*

PUZZLE RELAY

You'll need five sponsors, a large gymnasium or field, and two new 25-piece children's jigsaw puzzles.
• Mark one box with an X, and mark the back of each piece from that puzzle with an X as well.
• Mark the other box with a Z, and mark each of the corresponding pieces with a Z.
• Mark 16 small envelopes with an X, place one piece from the X puzzle in each envelope, and seal it. Put the nine remaining pieces back in their box.
• Do likewise for the 16 pieces from the Z puzzle.
• Set up a big table at home base, then designate five checkpoints about 30 to 40 yards away from home.
• Of the 32 envelopes, give to each of four sponsors four X envelopes and four Z envelopes.
• To the fifth sponsor give the two puzzle boxes.
• Assign one sponsor to each checkpoint; the sponsor with the boxes goes to checkpoint five.

Now divide all the kids into an X team and a Z team. Choose a team captain for each team, then divide both teams into four equal subteams.

While the two team captains stay at home base, each subteam makes the round of the checkpoints in a different order:

Group A: 1-2-3-4-5
Group B: 4-1-2-3-5
Group C: 3-4-1-2-5
Group D: 2-3-4-1-5

The entire subteam must travel to and from each checkpoint together. The sponsor at each checkpoint gives each subteam a task to perform;

83

upon completion of the task, the sponsor gives the group one envelope for their team's puzzle. Here are sample tasks:

Checkpoint 1: Sing one verse of "Pharaoh Pharaoh."

Checkpoint 2: Recite John 3:16 backward.

Checkpoint 3: Sing "Deep and Wide" with hand motions while running in place.

Checkpoint 4: Form a six-person pyramid and recite the Pledge of Allegiance.

Checkpoint 5: (captain only) Do an impersonation of Elvis.

Each subgroup must return to home base after each checkpoint and hand the envelope to their captain. The captain will put the unopened envelopes on the table. When all the envelopes are in and the entire team—that is, all four subteams—has returned to home base, the team captain must then go to checkpoint five, complete the task given, and return to home base with the box containing the remaining pieces to the team's puzzle. The envelopes are then torn open and the puzzle is completed by the team. The first team to complete its puzzle wins. *Gary Tapley.*

Pyramids by Braille

In this relay a blindfolded player must crawl 10 or 20 feet to where six Styrofoam cups lie. He must stack

them up, pyramid fashion, before returning to his team and passing the blindfold off to a teammate. You, meanwhile, knock down each pyramid for the next players.
John Krueger

Tapehead

Whether you play this game as a relay or a watch-and-cheer game, it's hilarious! Students wrap up their partner's head completely (obviously, making

sure player can breathe) with masking tape, sticky side out. Then, in competition, the partial mummies run or crawl to an area

where a variety of small, light objects are spread. They must lower their heads onto objects, "stick" 'em, then bring them back to where their partners remove the items and send their mummies back for another trip. The pair or team whose tapehead fetches the most items in a given amount of time wins.

Here are some common articles easily picked up by a tapehead: egg cartons, Styrofoam cups, plasticware, milk cartons, construction paper, shoe boxes, string, pie tins, paper clips, rubber bands, cotton balls, marshmallows, small stuffed animals, pencils, Q-Tips, inflated balloons, and paper plates. *Steve Bridges*

Blanket Ride Relay

This is a relay in which one team member rides on a blanket pulled by teammates. The rider is positioned on the blanket, sitting cross-legged and holding on tightly. Other team members line up behind the starting line. The first player in line grabs a corner of the blanket and assumes a pulling position. At the signal, the player begins pulling the blanket across the room, around a marker at the far end, then back to the starting point where the next player in line takes over. The blanket must be pulled completely over the line before the next team member may pull. The first team to complete all rounds wins. Obviously this game works best on a slick floor.

• **Paper Route.** In Paper Route the rider on the blanket is given an armload of newspapers to deliver as he is being pulled around the room. Cardboard boxes or trash cans can be used as houses along the way, and the papers must be tossed accurately into them for points.

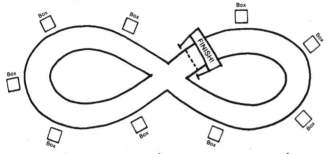

A variation is to have teammates seated in chairs along the route, but far enough away that the paper would have to be tossed a good distance. The person in the chair must catch the paper without leaving the chair, or the paper deliverer on the blanket must make another pass and try again. For added excitement, have several teams going at once with their courses criss-crossing or going in opposite directions. *Norman "Beetle" Bailey and David Washburn*

CIRCLE THE BROOM RELAY

Give each team a broom. The team captain holds the broom while teammates line up 20 feet away at a starting line. One by one, teammates run to their captain, grab the broom, and quickly circles it 10 times. Then they hand the broom back to the captain, return to the starting line, and tag the next teammate who does the same. The first team to complete the relay wins. It's great fun to watch dizzy players trying to get back to the starting line.

BUMPER BOX RELAY

Give each team one large refrigerator box and one safety helmet. One player from each team must put on the helmet and get inside the team box, open end down. She is to race to a goal line with the help

of teammates who yell directions. Teammates are not allowed to run with the players in the boxes; they must stay behind the starting line. Since players in the boxes can't see, they run into each other, go the wrong way, trip, and get lots of laughs. Enhance the competition by letting teams decorate their boxes with wild colors, team names, etc.

CATERPILLAR RELAY

Divide the group into equal teams. Have one kid from each team pull a sleeping bag over his or her head and race, relay style, to a far line and back. Since runners can't see where they are going, teammates shout directions to them. Each person on the team must run the relay. The first team to finish is the winner.

If you prefer, you can have kids crawl in their sleeping bags (like caterpillars) which is slower, but safer. You may want to give the runners helmets.

CLOTHESPIN RELAY

String a clothesline from one end of the room to the other, shoulder high for the average person. Place clothespins on the line. Teams line up facing the line. The object is to run to the line, remove one clothespin with your teeth (no hands), and bring it back to the team. All team members do the same in relay fashion. *Sue Broadhurst*

DRIVING PIGS TO MARKET

Give each team one pencil, ruler, stick, or broom handle and a pig, which is really a lemon, plastic soda bottle, potato or raw egg. Teams line up at the starting line. At the signal, the first player pushes the pig to the goal and back using the stick. That player passes the stick to the teammate who is next in line, and so on until all have run. The team that finishes first wins. Other variations are to set up an obstacle course or to push with noses instead of sticks.

GRAB BAG RELAY

Teams line up single file behind a line. A paper bag containing individually wrapped, edible items is placed on a chair at the opposite end of the room. At the signal, the first person in line runs to the chair, sits down, reaches into the bag (without looking), pulls out an item, unwraps it, and eats it. When she has swallowed the entire contents of her item, the official okays it, and she runs back to the starting position and the next contestant takes his turn. Each contestant must eat whatever is grabbed out of the bag. The first team to finish the contents of the grab bag wins. Suggestions for the grab bag:

- pickles
- cereal
- candy
- jar of baby food
- can of pop (warm)
- peanut butter sandwich
- box of Cracker Jack
- piece of cream cheese (wrapped in wax paper)
- olives
- onions
- carrots
- green onion
- orange
- walnut

Norman "Beetle" Bailey and Ed Bender

HUMAN WHEELBARROW

In this relay game, kids pair up. One partner walks on his hands while the other partner holds up his feet, as in a wheelbarrow race. Contestants must maneuver through an obstacle course. Penalize missed obstacles. The first to finish wins.

Or try it this way: Get a six-inch wheel and place a 12-inch length of pipe through it. Player A grabs both sides of the pipe, and Player B lifts Player A's legs and pushes him like a wheelbarrow to a goal. *Roger Disque*

WHEELBARROW EAT

Each wheelbarrow pair has a trail of food items, such as bread or grapes on the floor, and the partner who is the wheelbarrow must follow the food trail and eat his way to the goal. The first team to do so is the winner.

WEIRD BARROW RACE

In this race the added difficulty is that the wheelbarrow (player A) pushes a volleyball along the ground with his nose. This can be done as a relay, with team members pairing off and pushing the ball around a goal and back. *Burney Heath*

BLIND WHEELBARROW RACE

This game is as much fun to watch as it is to play. You need two large wheelbarrows, two identical obstacle courses, and three people on each team.

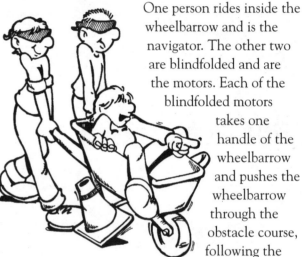

One person rides inside the wheelbarrow and is the navigator. The other two are blindfolded and are the motors. Each of the blindfolded motors takes one handle of the wheelbarrow and pushes the wheelbarrow through the obstacle course, following the directions of the navigator. Be ready for some crashes and spills! You can run heats to determine the winner, or you can use a stopwatch to determine the best time. Be sure to play this game on a soft surface like a grass field. *Dan Scholten*

WHEELBARROW GLADIATORS

The object of Wheelbarrow Gladiators is to be the first team to have participants complete all 10 stations.

You need three teams, three wheelbarrow chariots, course markers, and a playing field set up with activities at 10 stations. To make the chariots, decorate industrial wheelbarrows with cardboard horse heads and rope tails. Secure a two-by-four piece of wood horizontally under the wheelbarrow's arms to enable two students to lift up the wheelbarrow and pull it along. A third teen sits inside the chariot on a carpet sample or blanket.

WHEELBARROW GLADIATORS

Game overview: Three players begin at the starting point and run to the first station, where they eat the Twinkies. The players waiting at the first station run to the second and complete their portion of the race. The race continues in this manner until the last station, which requires the participation of all team members.

Station	Activity	Materials Needed	Participants
1	**Twinkie-Eating Contest.** *Three teammates wolf down ten Twinkies.*	30 Twinkies	3 gals
2	**Baby Care.** *Arriving players diaper the waiting players and feed them each a bottle.*	9 filled baby bottles 3 chairs 3 diapers 6 diaper pins	3 guys
3	**Balloon Shave.** *One player blows up a balloon, another smears on shaving cream, and the third shaves the balloon with a razor. If the balloon pops, the team must start the activity again.*	9 balloons 3 razors 3 chairs 3 bibs 3 cans shaving of cream paper towels water table	3 guys/gals
4	**Down a Jar of Pickles.** *The three teammates remove the pickles from the jar with forks and snarf 'em.*	3 jars of pickles 9 forks table	3 guys/gals
5	**Toilet Paper Mummy.** *Two players wrap one player with toilet paper until the two rolls are completely used up.*	6 rolls of toilet paper	2 guys/1 gal
6	**Lick and Stick.** *Two players lick Lifesavers and stick them to the third teen's face. Every piece of candy must be stuck on simultaneously for the team to pass to the next station.*	3 packages of Lifesavers 3 chairs	3 guys/gals
7	**Egg Jump Rope.** *Two players twirl the jump rope while one player jumps, throws the egg into the air (higher than the jump rope at its peak), and catches the egg without breaking it.*	3 jump ropes 3 eggs (and many extras)	3 guys/gals
8	**Chug-a-Jug.** *All three players must finish off the jug of juice using straws.*	3 gallons of juice 9 straws	3 guys/gals
9	**Basket Shoot.** *All three players must make a basket.*	3 basketballs 3 small trash cans	3 guys/gals
10	**Pyramid.** *Every team member must be on or under at least one other player when making the pyramid.*	none	all participants

Set up the stations in accordance with the chart on page 87 (or substitute your own ideas). Students are assigned to each station where they take over the wheelbarrow from the previous three participants. Some activities are best suited for all guy, all gal, or mixed groups.

At the signal the first set of players from all three teams pull their wheelbarrows from the starting point to the first station, where they devour Twinkies. After completing the activity, the three gals waiting at the first station take the wheelbarrow and race to the second station, where they diaper and feed the three guys who are waiting. When they have finished, the diapered guys take the wheelbarrow to the third station and continue.

All three teams are racing from station to station at once, causing considerable chaos and excitement. To add to the fun, play gladiator-style music, and have the students riding in the wheelbarrow dress like gladiators. They must pass the costume from rider to rider. *Tim Laycock*

INNER TUBE RELAY

Same-sex players pair up and race from a starting line to a pile of inner tubes. Partners must squeeze through the tube together, starting with the tube over their heads and working it down. The first pair to finish wins. Inner tubes should be regular auto tire size, not super small or very large.

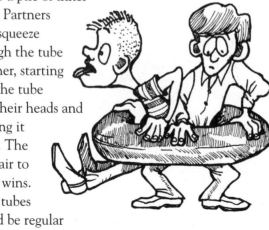

INNER TUBE ROLL RELAY

This challenging game can be played indoors or out. Divide the group into teams with an even number of people on each team. Then each team has its members pair up. If a team does not have an even number, someone can go twice. The first pair from each team stands behind the starting line. A large inflated inner tube (preferably a bus or truck tire inner tube) is placed on the floor between them. At the signal the pair must stand the tube up and together roll it around a chair and back to the starting line without using their hands. If the inner tube falls while they are rolling it, they must come back to the starting line and begin again. They are not allowed to kick the inner tube along in a lying down position. When the pair successfully completes their round trip, the next pair places the tube flat on the floor and without using their hands they stand it up and "keep on tubin'." The first team to have all of its pairs successfully complete the relay is the winner. *Samuel Hoyt*

TUBE-A-LOON RELAYS

The Tube-a-loon Relay can be done any one of three ways, depending on the agility of the group involved.

Easy Version. Place a number of balloons at one end of a room or route and the team members at the other. Place several inner tubes between the players and balloons. At the whistle a team member gets a balloon and returns to the line and the next person repeats the process. The players must step through the inner tubes both going and coming.

Intermediate Version. This game is a bit more difficult and cozy. Team members pair up. At the sound of the whistle, the pair (holding hands) must go through the tubes without letting go of each other, pick up a balloon and place it between them (no hands after that), and return to the line going back through the inner tubes. It is important to have tubes that are large enough and not overly inflated.

Professional Version. This time put a balloon at the end of the room for each team member. At the whistle the first person goes through the tubes, gets a balloon, and returns back through the tubes.

Leaving the balloon at the starting line, he then picks up the next person (not literally, but holding hands) and repeats the course. The process is repeated until the entire team is going after the last balloon. Team members are not allowed to break hands at any time. *Doug Dennee*

KNEE KNOCK RELAY

Have teams form a straight line. A pop bottle filled with water and frozen is given to the first member of each team. The object is to have players place the bottle between their knees and pass it to the person behind without using their hands. This works best at beach parties or swimming parties where everyone is in shorts.

MATTRESS RELAY

The group is divided into two teams. Half the team members lie flat on their backs on the floor, side by side, alternating head to foot.

The other half of the team is transported one at a time on top of the mattress—which is passed by the hands and feet of the kids on the ground. When the first mattress rider gets to the end of the line, she jumps off so the mattress can be passed back to the beginning so another person can get on. If anyone falls off, she must get back on the mattress where she fell off. The object is to see which group can transport its team members from one end to the other the quickest.

This works best when the kids laying down are bigger and stronger. The lighter the riders, the better. *Jerry Sprout*

MATTRESS RACE

Divide into two teams. Each team selects a number of sleepers from its members (you determine the number for your group). This is a relay game in which the members of the teams carry all the sleepers (one at a time) a distance of approximately 100 feet from the starting point across the finish line

on a mattress. The mattress must be carried shoulder high or the group has to start over. The first team to get all its sleepers across the finish line is the winner.

MATCHBOX RACE RELAY

Using only their noses, pairs of teammates pass an empty box of matches to the next pair in line.

MONOCLE RELAY

In this relay teams line up single file. The first person on each team places a quarter on his eye, squints, and holds it there like a monocle, using only his facial muscles. He runs to a given point and back and hands it off to the next teammate in line. Players can't use their hands after the quarter is in place. If a player drops the quarter, he must start over at the starting line. The first team to finish is the winner.

NEWS RELAY

Teams line up on one end of the room. On the other end, hang the front page of the newspaper, several clippings, or a whole newspaper. Prepare questions on the news stories ahead of time. You ask a question and one person from each team runs to the newspaper and locates the correct answer. The first to shout it out wins a point for the team. Continue until everyone has had a turn. *Don Snider*

RACING SLICKS RELAY

This is a good outdoor game for picnics. Teams form straight lines. The first person is given a 25-pound block of ice to ride down a grassy slope and carry back. Arms and legs may be used for propulsion. All members of the winning team are awarded an ice cube. *Ralph Moore*

BARBERSHOP RELAY

Kids are divided into teams and each team is arranged girl-boy, girl-boy, etc. Each boy is given a balloon. The first girl of each team is given a can of shaving cream and a razor minus blade. At the signal, the first boy blows up his balloon, ties it, and places it under his chin. The girl covers it with shaving cream and then shaves it. When finished she passes the razor and shaving cream to the next girl. The second boy blows up his balloon and the process is repeated. The first team finished wins.

Or skip the balloons. Each member of the team must run to a barber chair, get lathered up, and receive a shave. First team to shave all members wins. *Jerry Summers and Henry Skaggs*

SKI RELAY

Construct skis out of plywood and nail old shoes (from Goodwill or the Salvation Army) to them. Divide your group into teams and each member of the team must put on the skis, ski to a pole, go around it, and return. Walking with skis is a riot to watch, and going around the pole is really tough with long skis. *Von Trutschler*

SKI FILL

At the starting line set up a small bucket of water for each team. At the opposite end of the room place a turn-around cone as well as an empty container. Give the first member of each team a paper or Styrofoam cup with a small hole in the bottom. On "Go!" the players must put on their skis, fill their leaky cups from the bucket, then ski their way to the cone, where they pour what remains of their water into the container. After they ski back to their own teams, the following players do likewise until one team's container is filled with water.

SKI PLUNGER TOSS

Seat a victim at the far end of the room from the relay starting line. The first player in each team must put on skis, pick up a plunger by the handle, grab a water balloon from a pile near each team, place the balloon in the plunger end, ski to a designated firing spot, and let fly at the victim (who, in all fairness to the shooters, must sit on her hands). Any skier who drops a water balloon en route

forfeits his shot and instead returns to his line to let the next teammate go. The winning team is determined however you like—the first to wet the victim, the most hits in the least time, etc.

This game is appropriate for "honoring" a special adult or student. And you may find that most of the balloons don't have enough velocity to pop when they hit the victim. But don't tell the victims that—let them sweat it out.

BALLOON RACQUET RELAY

The object of this relay is to ski the length of the course (either around the cone or through an obstacle course), all the while keeping a balloon in the air with a racquet (tennis, badminton, racquetball, etc.). *Robert Marin, Jr.*

SKI TEAM RELAY

Make four pair of skis, similar to the one shown in the diagram. Make them about five feet long from

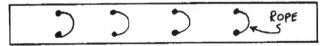

¾-inch pine boards. Drill holes one inch from each side at one-, two-, three-, and four-foot intervals. Put sturdy string or rope through each pair of holes and tie each off, leaving enough room for players to slip their feet under the loops. Two teams can participate at the same time during each relay (four teammates per set of skis).

LAWN SKIING

For those who long for the mountain slopes or whose lakes and rivers may be dry, try this. Acquire several pairs of water skis and remove the fins from the undersides. Get the necessary number of tow ropes or just plain rope (you'll need at least 40 feet), and begin your races. Local school or park lawns (just watered) provide a slick surface, and kids pulling the ropes provide the power. Many variations are possible using slalom skis, skim boards, inner tubes, etc., and other surfaces besides grass are suitable. Events can range from slaloms to marathons. *Gary Liddle*

SKIPROPE-ISSY-DISSY RELAY

Each member of the team skips rope from the starting line to a designated point where he lays down the rope and picks up a bat. He puts the small end of the bat to his forehead and with the large end on the ground spins around five times. He then picks up the skip rope and skips back to the starting line however erratically. Players take turns until everyone is back in starting position. The first team to finish is the winner. *Bill Flanagan*

SIX-STEP RELAY

Teams line up single file about 15 feet from a basketball goal (they would be standing at the foul line).
• At the signal, the first two people of each team leapfrog to a designated spot.
• The first player in line continues on by rolling a peanut with his nose to another designated spot.
• The second player goes back to the front of the line.
• The first player puts a Ping-Pong ball in a spoon and walks to another designated spot.

• He takes a basketball and goes to the back of the line. His team members stand in a straight line and spread their legs apart. The first player rolls the basketball through the entire team's legs and runs to the front of the line to catch up with the basketball.
• Once he gets ahold of it, he must make a basket.
• He goes to where a small glass of pop is waiting, drinks it, and burps.

When this whole routine is finished, the next player in line goes through the whole process. The winning team is the one that has every member complete each event and finishes first. *Gary Armes*

SOCK RACE

Each participant is blindfolded and seated in a small circle within reach of a huge pile of worn-out socks. Each participant is given a pair of thick gloves to put on. At the signal, each participant tries to put as many socks on his or her feet as possible in the time allowed (about two minutes). *William C. Moore*

STAGGER BAG RELAY

Teams of equal number line up single file. Each line is given one zipped-up sleeping bag. At the signal, the first person in line puts the sleeping bag over his head and is spun around three times. He then proceeds to stagger and stumble to the opposite line. Audience and team members may cheer to assist the staggerer to find the right way, but they may not touch him. When he crosses the end line, he takes the bag off and runs back, carrying the bag with him. Next person in line takes her turn. This continues until the team completes all turns. The first team finished is the winner.

THIMBLE RELAY

Create teams. Give players a straw, which they hold upright in their mouths. Players pass a thimble using their straws. The team that gets the thimble to the end of the line first is the winner.

91

THREE-LEGGED RACE

Form teams and have teammates pair up. Give each pair a piece of twine. Have them stand side by side, tie together the two touching legs, and race to a goal and back.

BACK-TO-BACK RELAY

Rather than tying two people together side by side, you tie two people together back-to-back. One of them runs forward and the other runs backward. When they reach the finish line, instead of turning around to run back, the one who ran forward now runs backward. Players should be tied together at the waist with a rope or belt. When one pair finishes, the next pair goes. First team to finish is the winner. *Burney Heath*

SEVEN-LEGGED RACE

Divide the kids into two teams. Have temmates pair off and get on their hands and feet backside down (crab position). With fabric scraps, tie a right arm to the left arm of each pair of kids. Have them race relay style to a set place and back again, one pair at a time. The first team to finish wins. *Jim Walton*

TOILET PAPER RELAY

Each team lines up single file and unwinds a roll of toilet paper over their heads and up and down the line. The team that has the smallest roll left after a set time limit is the winner, or the first team to use up the entire roll wins.

WADDLE TO THE BOTTLE

Create teams and give each teammate a coin. One by one, players from each team must race 15 or 20 feet to a plastic bottle with a thin neck. Players are to drop the coin into the bottle without using hands. If the coin is dropped along the way, the player must start over. Teammates may begin the relay only after the previous teammate has successfully dropped the coin in the bottle. The first team to have all players deposit the coin wins.

BACK BALL RELAY

This game can be played indoors or out. Divide the group into teams of six or more, then each team's members pair up. If a team does not have an even number, someone can go twice. The first pair from

each team stands behind the starting line. A basketball or volleyball is placed between them just above the belt line as the pair stands back to back. The object of the relay is, with their arms folded in front of them and not using their elbows, to carry the ball around a chair (about 30 feet away) and back again without dropping it. If the ball is dropped, the pair must start over. When the pair successfully completes their round trip, the next pair places the ball between their backs and does the same thing.

The first team to have all of its pairs successfully complete the relay are the winners.

This is more difficult than it may sound. The pair must really communicate and work together or else they will drop the ball and start over again and again. If a pair cannot do it after several attempts, have them go to the back of the line so that the rest will have a chance to try it.

• **Back-Up Relay.** Have two people race to a point, face each other, and hold their arms straight up in the air. Someone from their team places a ball between them. They must simultaneously make a 360-degree turn without the ball falling to the ground. They return to their team and the next two people do the same. If the ball falls, they must start over. *Samuel Hoyt*

ICE CREAM CONE RELAY

In this relay teams can compete against each other or against the clock for the best time. Divide students into teams and position the students so that half are at one end of the playing area and half are at the opposite end. The first two players at one end are each given one cone. A Nerf ball, slightly larger than the cone, is placed on the first runner's cone.

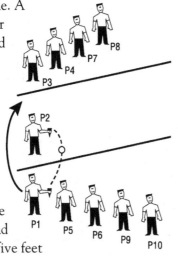

The first player stands behind the start line, facing the far end of the field, ready to throw the ball from the cone. The second player may stand approximately four to five feet out, facing the first player ready to catch the ball.

At the signal, the first player tosses the ball from the cone to the second player who must catch the ball on the cone without using any hands. The penalty for using hands to catch the ball is starting over. After the ball has been caught, the throwing player runs past the catching player, turns, and catches the ball. In this way they work down the field. When one player passes the goal line at the far end of the field, both runners hand their cones to the next set of two, and play reverses back down the field and continues until the relay is finished.

Mark Christian, Abbie Peyton, Kim Rochon, Tim Footdale, and Jody Tripp

BLOW CUP RELAYS

Give each team a 15-foot piece of string with a sliding paper cup on the string (see diagram). The string is held taut, the paper cup is placed at one end, and the team lines up single file.

At the signal each player must blow the cup to the other end (hands behind the back) and then push it back to the start for the next player. The first team to finish wins.

For this variation, tape two Styrofoam cups together, bottom to bottom, punch a hole in the center of the two connected bottoms, and thread it onto a piece of string.

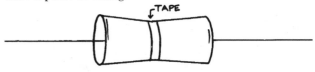

The string is then connected to two stationary objects and pulled tight. Each team lines up, half on one end of the string and half on the other end. The first person blows the cup along the string to the other end, and the person on that end blows it back to the other end and so on, until everyone has gone. The first team to finish is the winner. You will need a string and cup for each team if teams compete all at once. Or you can have the teams go one at a time, and time them with a stopwatch. Fastest time wins.

Another way to do this would be to have two teams line up on each end of the string, with the cup positioned in the middle. On "Go!" the first two players run out to the center and start blowing, trying to outblow their opponent. A whistle is blown and they stop, run back to their team, and two new players take over wherever the other two leave the cup. The object is to blow the cup as deeply as possible into the other team's territory. The game ends when the cup reaches the end of the line or after all the players have had their turn. The team that ends up with the cup in its territory loses the game. *Gail Beauchamp and Tom Bougher*

BROOM WHIRL RELAY

All teams line up in a straight line and the first person of each team is given a broom. The first and the second person hold on to the broom with both hands. On start the pair must turn around in place, so that they start face-to-face, then go side-to-side, back-to-back, side-to-side, then face-to-face. Both individuals must hold on to the broom at all times. Then the second and third person repeat what the first and second person did, and so on until the broom reaches the last person. The last person must then run to the front of the line, with the broom, and repeat the process with the first person. The team to do this first wins.

One variation is to have each pair turn around 10 times before going to the next person. *Bill Flanders*

BROOM JUMP RELAY

Divide into teams. Pairs should stand side by side facing forward. The first pair on each team is given a broom. At a signal, the pair must each grab one end of the broom, hold it just above the floor, and everyone in the line must jump over the broom as they run by. When the pair reaches the back of the line, they must pass the broom back to the front of the line. This is done by hands only—no throwing. Then the second pair repeats the process. The game is won by the first team with the original pair again heading the team. *Louis F. Stumpf*

CASTER RACE

Get several mechanic's casters (the type they lay on and slide under cars with). Line teams up and have races. Kids lay on the casters and race by propelling with hands only, feet only, on their backs, etc. This is best on cement floors. *Roger Disque*

CLOTHESPIN HOPPING RELAY

Divide the group into at least two relay teams. Each team should have no more than six members, otherwise this will get boring for those awaiting their turn. The object of this game is to hop in a burlap or cloth bag up to a clothesline that is full of clothespins, jump up and grab a clothespin with your teeth, and then hop back to your team. The first team that has each member complete this task is the winner. *Bill Calvin*

COIN, BOOK, AND BALL RELAY

This relay is absolutely hilarious to watch. Divide the group into teams. Each team is given one quarter, one tennis ball (or any kind of ball that size), and a book. The idea of the relay is to balance the book on your head, hold the quarter in your eye, and place the ball between your knees, then walk to the finish line. No hands are to be used to help in any way. It's not as easy as it sounds, and makes people look very awkward. *Ora Barker*

DEUCE TO ACE HOP

Divide the group into at least two relay teams. The object of this game is to hop in a burlap or cloth bag up to a deck of cards, pick out the deuce of a particular suit, and hop back to your team. The next person picks out the three of the same suit and the game continues until one team has brought back to its starting line an entire suit of cards. To add spice to this game, include a pair of work gloves that must be worn while shuffling through the cards in search of the desired card. This game can be played by using skateboards rather than a bag. *Bill Calvin*

ELASTIC BAND RELAY

In preparation for this game, cut strips of inch-wide elastic three feet long. Overlap one inch and stitch on a sewing machine. The result will be a large elastic circle.

Break the group into teams of eight to 12 players. Supply each team with an elastic band. At the starting signal, the first player brings the band over his head and body before passing it on to the next player on the team. The first team to have all the players pass the elastic band over their bodies is the winning team.

Variations may have the players passing the elastic band up from the feet, or pairs passing the band over both bodies at once. *Prudence Elliot*

FEATHER RELAY

Divide into teams and give each team a box of small feathers. (Mallard or duck breast feathers are best. If all else fails, visit a fly-tying shop.) There should be one feather for each member of the team. At the signal, the first person on the team blows (through the air) his feather the length of the room and into a small box. At no time may he touch the feather. He may blow an opponent's feather in the opposite direction if the opportunity arises. The race continues until the team has all their feathers in the box, one at a time. This race can be doubly exciting if done on hands and knees. *Randall Newburn*

HAND-IN-GLOVE RELAY

This is a relay game in which the teams stand in line and pass a pair of gloves from one end to the other. Use winter gloves, rubber kitchen gloves, or large work gloves. The first person puts the gloves on, then the next person takes them off and puts them on himself. Each person takes the gloves off the person in front of him and puts them on himself. All fingers of the hand must fit in the fingers of the gloves. *Lee Weems*

HANGER RELAY

This is a relay game for two or more teams. You will need one coat hanger per person. Bend the hangers (the hook part) slightly so that they are more straight. Take some kite string and tie it around each person, through the middle of the hanger and just under the armpits. The hanger should be hanging on the person's back. Then make a ring out of another hanger. Any size will do—the smaller the

ring, the harder the game becomes. (You'll probably need some pliers to bend the hanger into a ring.) Line the teams up and, in relay fashion, pass the ring from person to person, using only the hanger on each person's back to pass it with. No hands are allowed. It takes real coordination. *Daniel Mullis*

HAPPY HANDFUL RELAY

This relay can be easily adapted for indoor or outdoor use. Assemble two identical sets of 12 miscellaneous items (i.e., two brooms, two balls, two skillets, two rolls of bathroom tissue, two ladders, etc.). Use your imagination to collect an interesting variety of identical pairs of objects. Place the two sets of objects on two separate tables.

Line up a team for each table. The first player for each team runs to his table, picks up one item of his choice, runs back to his team, and passes the item to the second player. The second player carries the first item back to the table, picks up another item, and carries both items back to the third player. Each succeeding player carries the items collected by his teammates to the table, picks up one new item, and carries them all back to the next player. The game will begin rapidly, but the pace will slow as each player decides which item to add to a growing armload of items. It will take increasingly longer for one player to pass his burden to the next player in line.

Once picked up, an item cannot touch the table or floor. Any item that is dropped in transit or transfer must be returned to the table by the leader. No one may assist the giving and receiving players in the exchange of items except through coaching. The first team to empty its table wins. *Ed Stewart*

HEADS UP

Here's a fun game that can be done as a team relay or simply for individual competition. You will need to make top hats for each participant or team, and you will need some string, ribbon (to tie the hats onto the players' heads), and plastic blocks or small lightweight balls.

Tie a block or ball to the end of each piece of string (about 30 inches long). Then tie the other end to the brim of each hat. The top should be open on each hat so that it

Open

String

Ribbon

Ball or plastic block

can be used to catch the ball. Tie the hats on the players' heads. Now, each person stands with his hands behind his back and tries to swing the ball into the top of the hat. He may do anything to get it in except use his hands. Hats can be made out of poster board and cardboard. *Dave Gilliam*

HULA HOOPLA

The Hula Hoop will never die. It has been around for quite a few years and should be around quite a few more. Here are a few Hula Hoop relays that can be a lot of fun. Divide into teams and run these relays in normal relay fashion. Each team should have a Hula Hoop.

1. Place a Hula Hoop on the floor 20 feet or so in front of each team. The object is for each player to run to the hoop, pick it up, and hula it around five or 10 times (you decide how many), drop it to the floor, and return to the line.

2. The object of this relay is for each person to take a Hula Hoop and hula while walking or running to a certain point 20 feet or so from the team and back. If the Hula Hoop drops, the player must stop, get the hoop going again, and continue.

3. Place the hoop 20 feet or so away from the team once again. The player must run to the hoop and try to pass it over her body without using her hands. In other words, she must stand in the hoop and work it up over her head with just feet, legs, arms, etc., but no hands.

4. This relay is similar to the one above only two or three people run to the hoop at the same time, and without hands, work the hoop up around their waists. Then they run to a point and back with the hoop in place around their waists. At no time may their hands be used to hold up the hoop.

Cary F. Smith

MAD RELAY

This is a different kind of relay race in which each contestant does something different. What the contestants do is determined by the directions in a bag at the other end of the relay course.

At the beginning of the race, each team is lined up single file. The first person on each team runs to the other end of the course to a chair. On the chair is a bag containing instructions written on separate pieces of paper. The contestant draws one of the instructions, reads it, and follows it as quickly as possible. Before returning to the team, the contestant must tag the chair. The contestant then runs back and tags the next runner. The relay proceeds in this manner, and the team that uses all of its instructions first is the winner. Here are a few examples of directions:

• Run around the chair five times while continuously yelling, "The British are coming! The British are coming!"
• Run to the nearest person on another team and scratch his or her head.
• Run to the nearest adult in the room and whisper, "You're no spring chicken."
• Stand on one foot while holding the other in your hand, tilt your head back, and count, "10, 9, 8, 7, 6, 5, 4, 3, 2, 1, blast off!"
• Take your shoes off, put them on the opposite feet, and then tag your nearest opponent.
• Sit on the floor, cross your legs, and sing the following: "Mary had a little lamb, little lamb, little lamb, Mary had a little lamb, its fleece was white as snow."
• Go to the last person on your team and make three different funny-face expressions, then return to the chair before tagging the next runner on your team.
• Put your hands over your eyes and snort like a pig five times and meow like a cat five times.
• Sit in the chair, fold your arms, and laugh hard and loud for five seconds.
• Run around the chair backward five times while clapping your hands.
• Go to a blond-haired person and keep asking, "Do blondes really have more fun?" until he or she answers.
• Run to someone not on your team and kiss his or her hand.

Larry Bennet

MESSAGE RELAY

Type out a crazy message on a piece of paper (one for each team). You could use one like this: "Mrs. Sarah Sahara sells extraordinary information to very enterprising executives."

Divide into teams and divide teams in half. Each half stands at opposite ends of the room. Give the message to the first person who opens it, reads it, wads it up, and throws it on the ground. She runs to the first person on the other side of the room and whispers it in his ear. Then he runs back and tells it to the next person and so on until the last person runs to the supervisor and whispers it to him. The team closest to the original message wins. Accuracy, not time, is most important, but they must run. *Richard Reynolds*

SHOE BOX RELAY

Here's a great idea for an Olympics Night. Obtain several shoe boxes, a high school track, and a referee. Divide the kids into teams. Have them place their feet into the boxes and then "hoof it" around the track. You should experience a hilarious situation. You may need plenty of replacement shoe boxes in case they wear out quickly. *Buzz Roberts*

SOCK TAIL RELAY

Make several sock tails, one for each team. A sock tail consists of a belt with a sock tied to it, with an orange in the end of the sock as a weight. The first person on each team puts on the tail with the sock hanging down behind him. Another orange is placed on the floor. At the signal, the player must push the orange on the floor to a goal and back, with the sock tail. If he touches it with his feet or hands, he must start over. The first team to have all team members complete this task wins. *John Simmons*

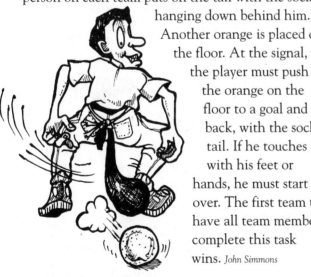

STILTS RELAY

Have someone who is handy with wood make up four pairs of stilts out of 2x2s (two pairs for each team). The foot-mount only needs to be 12 to 18 inches off the ground. Most kids will be able to walk on them with ease. Just line the teams up relay style and let 'em go. The first team to go to the goal and back on stilts (one at a time) wins. *Roger Disque*

SUCKER RELAY

Teams line up. Each person has a straw. A piece of paper (about four inches square) is picked up by sucking on the straw and carried around a goal and back. If you drop the paper, you must start over. Each person on the team must do it. First team to finish wins.

MARBLE SUCKING RELAY

For this game divide your group into several teams. Give each person a plastic straw and a paper cup. The first person on each team gets a marble in his cup. The object is to suck the marble up with the straw and drop it into the next person's cup. If the marble drops on the floor, the team must start over at the beginning. The first team to get the marble to the last person on the team wins. *Judy Groen*

WAGON RELAY

For this team relay, you will need to obtain the use of one or more wagons (the type that most kids have, but not too small). Each team pairs off and a pair at a time, one person sits in the wagon and uses the handle to steer while the other person pushes her around a slalom course. When one pair finishes, the next begins, and the first team to have everyone complete the course wins.

A variation of this is to have one person ride in the wagon, just sitting there doing nothing, while the other person holds on to the handle and uses it both to steer and to push the wagon backward through the course. It's not easy. *Sam Walker*

Cotton Ball Race

This is a good indoor relay game. Divide into teams, and provide each team with a number of cotton balls in a container such as a dish or pan. Each team also gets a spatula and an egg carton.

At the signal, the first person on each team picks up a cotton ball with the spatula, then tries to keep it balanced on the spatula while running to a goal and back. Of course, if players move too quickly, they will drop the cotton ball and must start over. When they return to their team with the cotton ball, they must place it in the egg carton in one of the unoccupied spaces. The first team to fill its egg carton wins. *Stan Lindstadt*

Gotcha Relay

Divide the group into two teams. Set up the room or field similar to the diagram below. Divide the teams so that they are about even in speed. Each team lines up single file behind its respective markers. The first players begin running around the track (in one direction only) just like in a regular relay race. On completing the lap, the runner tags the next player who takes off in a similar fashion.

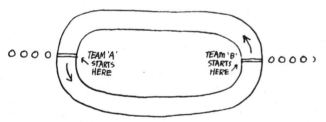

The object of the game is to try and tag the runner of the opposing team. The teams continue to run the laps until a person is finally caught. The team that catches the other first is the winner.

This can also be played piggyback, on tricycles, hopping on one foot, or whatever. *Brian Fullerton*

Piggyback Balloon Poke

Mark off several lanes on the ground, using tape or lime. At even intervals along each lane, securely fasten a balloon on the ground.

Players pair off, with one person designated as carrier and the other as rider, piggyback style. The rider gets a long, pointed (not too sharp) stick, like a broom handle. The carrier is blindfolded.

On a signal, they start down their lane. The object is for the rider to break the balloons with the stick by poking them as they walk by. The rider will have to give the carrier directions. After each round, replace the balloons and do it again with new contestants. Be sure kids avoid stabbing each other in the feet. *David Washburn*

Chariot Race Relay

Divide teams into groups of three. The first group of three from each team runs the relay, tags the next group of three, and so on. The two strongest people from the first group crisscross and lock arms and have the lightest person sit on their arms. The group of three races to a goal and back. The next group of three should be ready to race off as soon as it is tagged by the first group of returning teammates. The team whose last group crosses the finish line first wins.

TP-Rip Relay

Each team selects four kids to participate in this relay of skill. One player walks backward toward a goal some 50 feet away, unrolling a roll of toilet

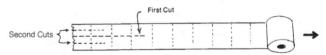

paper. Another person follows him with a pair of scissors and cuts the roll in half, lengthwise, without breaking the TP anywhere. Two more kids follow him, each cutting a half in half. The first team to reach the goal and have four separate thin rolls of toilet paper wins.

SUPERHERO RELAY

Here's a game you can play next time you're doing a lesson on heroes. You'll need two "phone booths" (be creative; a couple of refrigerator boxes will work), two dolls, several tables, two masks, and two pairs of high-topped tennis shoes.

Divide the group into two teams. Line them up about 50 feet away from the phone booths. The first two kids on each team run to their team's phone booth, go inside, and put on the mask and the "super-powered" shoes. Each runs to another room where she saves a baby (doll) from a burning building. Next she takes the baby to a hysterical mother, puts a hand over her heart, and says the Pledge of Allegiance to the flag while the mother hums a patriotic tune. From there,

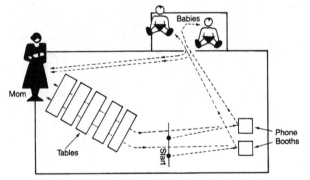

she tunnels under the earth (crawls under the tables) and flies back to the phone booth. (This is done by having four people carry her in the flying position.) Finally, she changes back into her street clothes and leaves the mask and shoes in the phone booths for the next two players. (Dolls must be returned immediately to the other room.) The first team to finish is the winner. *Rick Wheeler*

FOOTBALL RELAY

Have kids pair up and race to a goal with a football

wedged between them, first chin-to-chin, then back-to-back, and finally side-to-side. In other words, each pair races three times. If the ball is dropped, the pair must start over on that particular lap. Variations: Use grapefruits or balloons.

FRISBEE ON THE RUN

Here's a relay game that involves Frisbee throwing and hard running. Divide your group into two teams and then divide each team in half. Line teams up opposite each other across the playing area. The first player throws a Frisbee to a teammate at the other end of the playing area. After throwing it, he must run and tag the person to whom the Frisbee was thrown. The receiving player cannot be tagged unless he is behind the team line on his side of the field. So if the first player throws the Frisbee inaccurately, the receiving player must go get the Frisbee and run back to his original position before being tagged. After being tagged, that person can throw the Frisbee back the other way and repeat the process. The object of the game is to have the two halves of the team switch ends of the field. The first team to do so wins. You can lengthen or shorten the playing area depending on the skill of group members. *Brian Fullerton*

FRISBEE RELAY

Divide the group into equally sized teams of five or six per team. Any number of teams can play at once. Each team will need a Frisbee. The playing area should have plenty of length, such as a road (without traffic) or a large open field. Each team should spread out in a line with players about 50 feet apart or so. The first person throws the Frisbee to the second, who allows the Frisbee to land. That person then stands where the Frisbee landed and throws it toward the third person, who throws it to the fourth, and so on. The object is to see which team can throw it the greatest distance in the shortest time. Award points for throwing it the farthest and for finishing first. For added fun, have the guys throw left-handed (or right-handed if they are left-handed). Footballs can be substituted. *Scotty Shows*

GOLFENNIS

Golfennis is merely a relay race that combines, what else, golf and tennis. Provide students with plenty of tennis balls, golf clubs (7 irons work best) and an open space (like a golf course or a football field). You can't play regular golf (tennis balls are too big to go in the little holes, for one thing), but you can

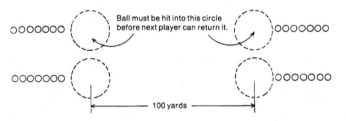

Ball must be hit into this circle before next player can return it.

← 100 yards →

have a relay race in which teams line up, with half the team on one end of the field, and the other half of the team on the other end of the field, about 100 yards away (see diagram). The first person in the line must hit the ball to the first person on the other half of her team as quickly as possible, and then that person returns it back to the original end of the field, and so on until all the players have hit. The first team to complete this task wins. It's a lot of fun, and when you're in a hurry, a tennis ball hit by a golf club can go anywhere. *Doug Larson*

TOOTHPASTE RACES

Give each team a new tube of toothpaste and a roll of toilet paper. The toilet paper is a track upon which to squeeze the toothpaste, so it's easy to clean up.

- **Race 1:** Go for the longest unbroken strand of toothpaste in a set length of time.
- **Race 2:** Lay out an obstacle course where players must run a strand of toothpaste over all sorts of objects. For a really spirited group, have the members of the team lie down and the toothpaste (without TP) can run across their faces, etc.
- **Race 3:** Go for the longest strand from one single new tube of paste per team!

Rob Moritz

BUNGEE RUNNING

For this boomerang foot race, borrow six or more bungee-jumping harnesses and bungee cords that allow for the different weights of your students. Anchor several bungee cords to something immovable, strap in as many willing teenagers, line them up, and say "Go!" Whoever runs farthest wins. Mark the winning distance with a Frisbee so the following sprinters have a visual goal to strive for.

Steve Duyst

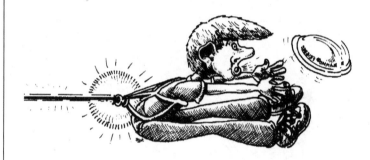

SOCCER AND HOCKEY GAMES

Brawls and rioting fans are optional in these variations of hockey and soccer. In a nutshell, these games generally involve two (or more) teams trying to do something resembling a ball or puck down the field (or ice or court or room) and into an opponent's goal.

BLIND SOCCER

This game is almost as fun to watch as it is to play. You need a large open floor space (a carpeted floor is preferable), two teams of five or more members per team, a couple of people to keep things going, two goals, blindfolds for each team member, and a large heavy ball (like a medicine ball). It may also be helpful for each player to have knee pads.

The object of the game is, like soccer, to put the ball through the goal. However, instead of running and kicking the ball, the players crawl on the floor and handle the ball with their hands. They should be told not to hold the ball for more than a second or two, and this is what the two officials are for. Many of the more intricate rules can be formed and reformed as you go along. For example, for the real heavyweights in the group, you might want to prohibit the ball from becoming airborne. *Lew Worthington*

BROOM HOCKEY

This game can be played with as many as 30 players or as few as five per team, but only six players from each team are actually on the field at one time. Give each team six brooms. Two teams compete by running onto the field, grabbing their brooms, and swatting at a volleyball placed on the center line. The goal is to push the volleyball across the opposing team's goal line. Each team has one goalie, who is the only player allowed to kick the ball or touch it with his hands and throw it out onto the playing field. If the ball goes out of bounds, the referee throws it back in. The rest of the players can only hit the ball with the broom. Score one point for each time the ball passes between goal markers. If you have a number of teams, limit play to three minutes each.

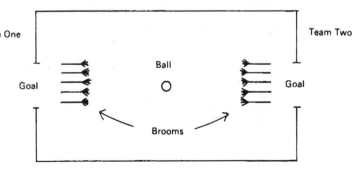

BROOM SOCCER

Arrange chairs in an oval, open at both ends.

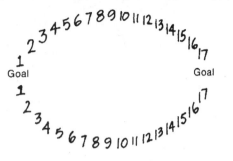

An equal number of kids sit on both sides. Each one has a number, with the same numbers on each team. To begin, the two number ones come to the center, and each is given a broom. A rubber or plastic ball is tossed into the middle, and the game begins. The two players try to knock the ball with the brooms through the opponent's goal. Each team is assigned one of the two open ends on the oval as their goal. The referee can at anytime shout out a new number, and the two players in the center must drop the brooms right where they are, and the two new players grab the brooms and continue. Play is in as long as the ball is in the oval. If it is knocked out, the referee returns it to play. Players in the chairs cannot intentionally touch the ball with their hands but may kick it if it is hit at their feet. *Jerry Summers*

CIRCLE SOCCER

Two teams get into one circle, half on one side and half on the other.

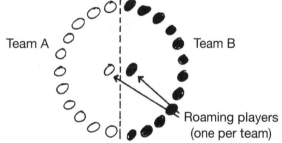

Team A   Team B

Roaming players
(one per team)

A ball is thrown into the circle and the players try to kick it out through the other team's side. If the ball is kicked out over the heads of the players, the point goes to the nonkicking team. If the ball is kicked out below the heads of the players, the kicking team gets the point. Hands may not be used at all, only feet and bodies. No one may move

out of position except one player per team who may kick the ball to his teammates if the ball gets stuck in the center. He may not score, however, or cross into the other team's territory. If the roaming player gets hit with the ball when kicked by the other team, the kicking team gets a point. *Ellis Meuser*

CRAB BALL

This is an active game for groups of 20 or more. All that is needed is a playground ball. Divide into four teams of equal size. Each team forms one side of the square. Players should then sit down on the floor and number off from one to however many players are on each team.

To begin the game the leader places the ball in the center and calls a number. All four players with that number crab walk out to the ball.

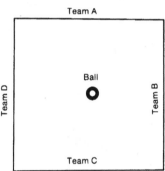

The object is to kick the ball out of the square, over the heads of one of the other teams. The team that had the ball go over their heads, gets a point.

The remaining members of the team must stay in place with their seats on the floor. They may block the balls coming at them either by kicking, using their bodies, or using their heads. They may never use their hands or arms. They also may try to kick it over the heads of an opposing team. The team gets the point if the ball gets past them this way too.

When the first team reaches 10 points, the game is ended and the lowest score wins. *Richard Boyd*

CRAB SOCCER

This game is played just like regular soccer except for two variations—the area of play should be smaller (like an indoor gym) and everyone except the goalies must move like a crab (on hands and feet with backs to the ground). Goalies can be on their knees, and they are the only ones who can use their hands to control the ball. Because of the reduced mobility of the players, it's best if you assign positions (forward, defense, left, right, etc.)

Marshall Shelley

CRAZY SOCCER

To add a little excitement to the ordinary game of soccer, try this adaptation. Use the basic soccer field, only with four goals instead of two (see diagram), and you divide into four teams instead of two. Team A plays against Team C while Team B is playing Team D. Two balls are in play but teams can only kick the ball for their own game.

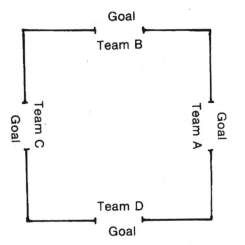

For even more variety you can combine teams so that Team A and C play Teams B and D. One team will defend A and C goals while the other team defends B and D goals. You can use one or two balls.

Another variation is to use the basic two-goal soccer field with a game between the guys and girls. Only the guys have to have their legs tied with rope two and a half feet long.

• **Crazy Crab Soccer.** Combine the rules and field layout of Crazy Soccer with the playing position of Crab Soccer (on hands and feet with backs to the ground). Play with a medicine ball.

Bill Rudge

CROAK BALL

This open field game is played just like soccer except that you use an old volleyball and croquet mallets turned sideways. The kids must push the ball with the mallets (no swinging the mallets to hit the ball). Put five to 10 students on each team, mark off

goals similar to soccer goals, and make up any other rules that you find necessary. Each team should have a goalie, but the goalie doesn't have to stay near the goal unless the other team is threatening to score.

Dick Moore

DONKEY SOCCER

This game is exciting and hilarious. To play, divide your group into four teams and place each team along one of the four sides of a square playing area. Place a soccer ball in the center of the square.

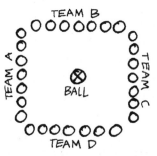

Each team chooses a donkey (player on the bottom) and one rider (player sitting on top of donkey's shoulders). The donkey is blindfolded and the rider then directs the donkey to the ball and gives direction as to which foot he should use to kick the ball. The object is for the donkey to kick the ball past one of the opposing teams. No points are awarded if the ball is kicked past one's own teammates. All four donkeys are trying at the same time.

Team members on the sides of the square may block the ball with their body, legs, and feet only (no hands). Points can only be made when the ball is kicked by a donkey. *Ben Smith*

FLIP FLOP HOCKEY

Here's a new way to put a pool table to use. You only need one billiard ball and six kids, each armed with one sport sandal (e.g., Teva). The heavier sandals work best.

Each player guards one pocket on the pool table with his sandal. The game begins when the server serves the ball, hitting it with the sandal. The ball must hit one cushion before any other player touches it. If a player touches it first, the server gets a free shot at that player's pocket. Once the ball is served, any player can hit the ball with his sandal until it goes into someone else's pocket. When a player successfully hits the ball into someone else's pocket, she scores a point.

If there are more than six youths who want to play, have them line up on one end of the table. Then, whenever a player scores a point, the defending player is knocked out of the game, goes to the end of the line, and the next player takes his place.

After each point is scored, all players rotate around the table so that everyone has a chance to play all the positions. The game can also be played as a team competition, with two teams each guarding three pockets. *John Davenport*

HURL HOCKEY

With one or two dozen plastic gallon milk jugs, you can play a fast, fun court game that's a mix of hockey and jai alai.

Cut the bottom out of the jugs in order to make a "glove" that also can hurl a ball toward a goal (see diagram).

One way to create a goal for Hurl Hockey is to split a Ping-Pong table in half and set each half at one end of the court; the goal is below the mid-stripe. Use masking tape to mark off an eight-by-six-foot goalie box in front of each goal.

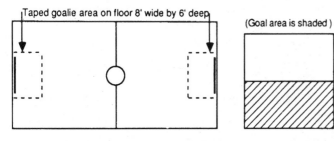

The game itself is played as hockey, though with a soft, baseball-size ball instead of a puck; the

ball can be scooped off the floor with the plastic gloves and passed or hurled at the goal.

Here are other details:
• Start the game with a hockey-type face-off.
• With the ball in their gloves, players can take only three steps, then must pass it or shoot at the goal.
• The ball can be touched only by the plastic glove, not by feet or by a player's free hand.
• Traveling (taking more than three steps) or out-of-bounds results in the nearest goalie putting the ball back into play.

Paul Holmberg

INNER TUBE SOCCER

This is a game of soccer, using the usual rules of the game, only substituting an inner tube for a normal soccer ball. It gives the game a new dimension. The tube should lie flat and the playing surface should be relatively flat and smooth.

Jerry Summers

LINE SOCCER

Here's a variation of soccer that is simple and a lot of fun. Divide your group into two equal teams. Each team numbers off successively (1, 2, 3, etc.) and lines up opposite each other on two sides of a playing area, about 30 feet apart. A gym floor will work fine. A line can be drawn in front of each team to designate the scoring area.

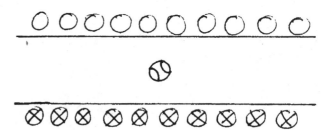

A ball is placed in the middle of the field and a referee calls out a number. The players on each team with that number run out to the ball and try to kick it through the opposite team (across their line). It cannot go over their heads. It must go between them, below the shoulders—below the waist if you prefer—in order to count as a goal. The defenders can catch the ball and toss it back in to their own player, or kick it back when it comes to them. After a minute or two, the referee can call out a new number. It really gets wild when you call out several numbers at once. *Christine Rollins*

INDOOR SOCCER

With a large, unfurnished room and a small (six-inch) soccer ball, you can stage your own indoor soccer tournaments. Adjust the rules to suit your own situation and to keep the game swift and safe. Divide large groups into teams of five—two teams play for two minutes, then are replaced by two new teams. Or keep 'em guessing with a tag-team variation—divide a big group into two teams, which divide themselves again into groups of five. At the whistle (blown at varying intervals) players stop playing where they are, run to their sideline, and tag a new group of teammates who resume play.

You can construct your own goals with just a few lengths of PVC pipe and some inexpensive cargo netting (see diagram).

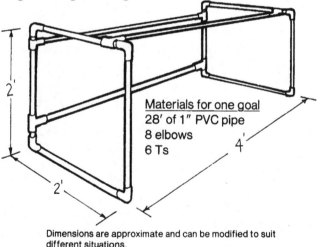

Materials for one goal
28' of 1" PVC pipe
8 elbows
6 Ts

Dimensions are approximate and can be modified to suit different situations.

So that you can disassemble them easily for storage, don't glue the pipe.

Dimensions are approximate and can be modified to suit different situations. *Jim Reed*

MONKEY SOCCER

For a fast-action outdoor game, designate a rectangular area of grass as a monkey soccer field, with a width of at least three feet per youth. Divide the youths into two teams, and provide one light-weight, volleyball-size ball. Here are the rules:

• The object of each play is for the team which has the ball to get it across the other team's end of the court.
• The ball must be kept either on the ground or else no higher off the ground than the height of the average player's knees.
• Players may propel the ball only by reaching down and hitting it with their hands (clenched fists or otherwise). While in motion, the ball may bounce off a player, even off her foot while the player is running, but the player may not intentionally kick the ball or strike it with any part of the body except the hands.
• Whenever the ball is kicked, or travels higher than a player's knees, or is held, it is placed on the grass where the foul occurred and put into play by the team that did not commit the foul.
• Whenever the ball leaves the court on a side, it is put into play at the point where it left the court by the team that did not touch it last.
• Teams may organize themselves in any way they desire to best protect their ends of the court. Each team earns one point when its players get the ball over the opposing team's end of the court. The winning team is the first one to score seven points. Substitute a garbage bag filled with inflated balloons and twist-tie it. Wrap the bag with masking tape to reinforce the bag, and use it for a soccer ball. *John Bristow*

OFFICIAL 43-MAN SQUAMISH

Here's a crazy game from an old edition of Mad magazine, and it is published here with permission.

Squamish will obviously be played on the Squamish field. The boundaries will be set by the Lunkhead.

Equipment? One, two, three, or four balls may be used. Two goals (known as the Furd), one on each end of the field are used. The object is simply to get the ball through the Furd.

Now for the rules:
• **The Ball.** The ball may be kicked (the Grotz), carried (the Emphle), or thrown (the Slam).

The Grotz must be done with the left foot (unless the player is left-footed, in which case it will be done with the right foot). If it is done with the right, this will be called a Rabble Grotz. Penalty: the loss of one man for two minutes.

The Emphle must be done with two hands. If done with one, this will be called a Rabble Emphle. Penalty: the loss of one man for one minute.

The Slam must be done with two hands. If done with one, this will be called a Rabble Slam. Penalty: the loss of one man for one minute.

• **The Tackle.** Tackling the player who is in possession of the ball is legal. This is called the Squamish Play, but must be preceded with the sound Org!

A man who Squamishes without an Org has committed a Rabble Squamish. Penalty: leave the game for one minute.

The Squamisher may not remove the ball from the player who has been Squamished. This must be done by another player.

An unnecessarily rough Squamish will force the ejection of the Squamisher.

• **Scoring.** The only legal way to get a ball through the Furd is with the Grotz. You may not use the Emphle or the Slam to score the Furd.

• **Goalies.** Two men, Gremles, may protect the Furd. If more than two Gremles are used, the Furd Gremles must remain out of the game for one minute.

• **Officials.** If an official, Tunken, calls a Rabble, the player who is Rabbled must report to the Rabble

Rouser. He will be told by the official timer, the Rabble Rouser, when to enter the game again. Overall supervision is by the Lunkhead. Tunkens and the Lunkhead have final word. The Lunkhead may make up his own rules as the game progresses.

Remember: Squamish is the true and elite sportsman's game and should be played with dignity (in accordance with the 43-man Squamish rules, in Mad magazine). *George H. Butler*

PEW SOCCER

Divide your students into one team per section of pews in your auditorium. One player from each team goes to the front of the auditorium; the rest find places under the pews in their section.

Here's what kids do under the pews: Starting at the front of the church, they move an inflated balloon to the back of the auditorium. If the balloon escapes through the sides, the person at the front must retrieve it and start the whole process again for his section. You can make the game more interesting by restricting how the students move the balloon—prohibit the use of hands, the use of legs, or whatever creative idea you think of. *Len Cuthbert*

PILLOW HOCKEY

The object of the game is to use pillowcases stuffed loosely with crumpled newspapers and tied off to hit, hockey fashion, a playground ball into a goal.

Lay the available pillows out on the court (an equal number on both sides of the court), then call for teams to select players, who run out to the court and immediately begin playing. When one side scores, call for new players from each team.

What makes this game fun is that it's difficult to hit the ball with much force, or even be too sure you hit it at all. Also, unlike Broom Hockey, players don't get smacked accidentally by wooden handles.

Keith King

RAINBOW SOCCER

This active game is played with two teams and 60 balloons (30 each of two colors). The balloons are mixed together and placed in the center circle of a regulation basketball court. The two teams line up on the end lines facing each other. One person from each team is the goalie who stands at the opposite end of the floor from his team, in front of a large container.

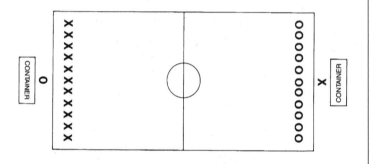

Players on each team try to kick (using soccer rules) their balloons to their goalie, who then puts them into the container behind him. To play defense, a team stomps and pops as many of the other team's balloons as possible. Play continues until all balloons are scored or popped. The team with the most goals wins. *Byron Harvey*

SANCTUARY SOCCER

This version of soccer allows you to play indoors and has a built-in equalizer to keep one team from dominating the game.

Play in a large room with all the chairs removed. You will need a Nerf (or some other soft) soccer ball and eight folding chairs. Line up four chairs at each end of the playing area for goals. Play regular soccer, with as many players as you wish. A goal is scored when the soccer ball hits one of the other team's chairs.

When points are scored the chair that is hit is removed from the goal of the team that was scored upon, and added to the chairs of the team who scored. Before the first goal, for example, the setup would look like this:

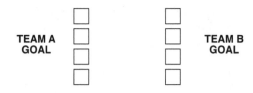

After Team B scores a goal, the setup would look like this:

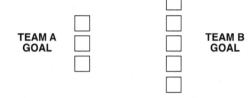

This way, the team that was just scored on will have an easier, larger target when the ball is back in play, while the other team has a smaller, more difficult target. Each team can have one goalie, as in regular soccer. *Larry Bong*

SHOE HOCKEY

Here's an active group game that should be played inside on a large smooth floor. It's a version of hockey, played with one shoe off and one shoe on. The one shoe off becomes the players hockey stick. The kids should be instructed to wear soft-soled shoes. A sock stuffed with cloth and tied closed becomes the puck. Each team should have five players at a time on the playing field. The floor should be marked to indicate boundaries, a mid-court line, and the goals on each end.

The rules are as follows:
• Each player uses one of his or her shoes as a hockey stick while wearing the other shoe and both socks.
• The puck may be stopped by any part of a person's body, but it may be propelled only by a player's hockey stick (shoe).
• The court is divided down the middle, with three members of each team restricted to their end of the room to guard the goal, while the other two members of each team are restricted to the opposing team's end of the room.
• The game is started by lining up the five players on one side (three of that side's team with two of the other team) facing the five on the other side, at least 10 feet away from the center spot. The referee places the puck on the center mark, backs away a

safe distance, and calls the game into play.

• Whenever the puck goes into the goal, even if it was hit by the wrong team, it scores a point for the offensive team.

• Fouls are called whenever a player hits another player with his shoe, knocks another player's shoe out of his hand, leaves his restricted area, or when a player propels the puck with anything other than the hockey stick. Players may be suspended from the game (placed in the penalty box) or the opposing team can simply take a free shot at the goal from mid-court.

John Bristow

SILLY SOCCER

Divide your group into two teams. In a large open field, place two pylons 100 to 150 feet apart. The object is to hit the opposing teams pylon with the ball. There are no boundaries, and the pylon may be hit from any direction. All other soccer rules apply. For added confusion with a large group, throw in a second ball. *Ron Elliott*

SIMPLE SOCCER

Here's a fantastic game that any number of kids can play. Mark a court in a large rectangle with the backcourt lines and center line clearly visible. Divide the players into two teams, one on each side of the court. Each team should then establish an offense and a defense—the offense stands on its side of the center line, the defense at the backcourt line.

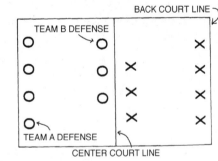

The object is to kick the ball past, over, or through the opposing team's backcourt line. However, no player may use hands or arms. The official puts the ball into play by throwing it into the court at the center line. Each successful score earns one point. The team with the most points in a certain time period wins. *Brett Wilson*

SOCCER ON PAPER

Here's a new way to play soccer that is best when played indoors. It's just like regular soccer, except that you give each person, including the goalie, a piece of paper to stand on and a particular place to put the paper. Players must keep one foot on the paper at all times. Scooting the paper is not allowed.

Be sure to scatter players from both teams evenly all over the playing area. Toss in a soccer ball and watch the fun. The effect is like a giant pinball machine. *Mitch Lindsey*

SOCKEY

Here's a great outdoor game that features elements from two popular games—soccer and hockey. In order to play, you will need a large playing field, two hockey sticks, a soccer ball, and a couple of medium-sized cardboard boxes for hockey goals. The playing field is laid out like the diagram below, with two marked circles approximately 10 feet in diameter at opposite ends of the playing field. The cardboard boxes (goals) should be another 10 or 15 feet away from the circles.

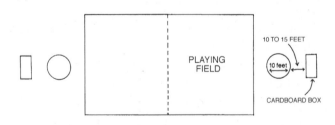

Divide the kids into two teams. Each team places one player with the hockey stick in the circle. She cannot leave the circle and no other player may enter the circle. The team must kick the ball to the circle containing their player. Hands cannot be used at any time. Once the ball is kicked into the circle, the player in the circle grabs the ball, places it, and tries to hit it into the cardboard box with the hockey stick. If she succeeds, she scores points for her team. If she misses, then it's a point for the opposing team. After each point is attempted, the ball is returned to midfield and play resumes. It's a good idea to rotate the player within the circle so everyone has a chance to score, and so that no one player can dominate the game. *Doug Newhouse*

SOLO SOCCER

When you don't have enough people for a regular soccer game, or even when you do, you might want to try this challenging variation. Arrange the players spread apart in a large circle. Mark a goal beside each player by putting two stakes in the ground about six feet apart. The object is to protect your own goal while trying to score through someone else's. The last person to touch the ball before it goes through the goal receives one point. The person who is scored upon loses a point. Goals should not be allowed that are kicked above the goalie's head. *Kathie Taylor*

←── GOAL MARKERS

THREE-LEGGED SOCCER

Pairs get their legs tied together like a three-legged race (including goalies), then get teamed up for soccer. One group played this game in the fall on a large tomato field with plenty of overripe tomatoes all over the playing area. Make sure kids are instructed to wear long pants. *Harry Heintz*

WALL HOCKEY

This is an indoor game that can be played by groups as small as six or as large as 50.

The playing area should be bounded on two sides by walls, where the players must line up in two

equal teams, one team along each wall (see diagram).

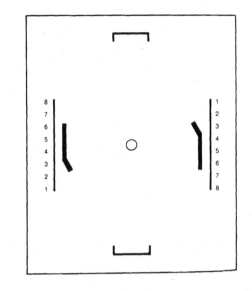

At the other two ends of the play area goals are set up, using street hockey nets, boxes, or chairs. The object of the game is to score the most goals by hitting the puck or ball into the opponent's net.

Players must count off in order, numbering themselves in one direction on one team and in the opposite direction on the other team. Each team is given a hockey stick (a broom will do if you use a larger ball).

To begin play, all players must place one hand on the wall behind them, and keep it there at all times during the game. Players on each team next gather to place their free hand on the hockey stick. Once everyone is holding the stick, the leader calls out a number, and the player from each team with that number takes his hand off the wall, grabs the stick, and goes out to face the opponent. The rest of the team members release the stick but must keep a hand on the wall. Failure to do so costs a player's team one point.

To make the game more interesting, call out other numbers during a play. The two players in the center must then drop their sticks where they are, return to their lines, and put a hand on the wall before the next player can go out. This also helps keep more kids in the game. With large groups of 50 or more, you may want to divide up into four teams—one pair with letters and one with numbers—and then call out numbers and letters alternately. *Brian Fullerton*

WHIFFLE HOCKEY

For indoor or outdoor fun, create your own hockey sticks and play with a Whiffleball. You'll need a Wiffleball, several old broom sticks, empty two-liter plastic soda bottles, and duct tape. Screw the broom sticks into the soda bottles and tape to secure.

Follow normal hockey rules, or make up your own. Variations can increase the fun—wear rollerblades while playing or substitute the Whiffleball with a thick-skinned balloon. *Keith Curran*

WINDBAG HOCKEY

A great way to play hockey in a small, confined area is to get teams down on all fours, and place a Ping Pong ball in the center. The teams must then blow the Ping Pong ball through their goals (a doorway or the legs of a chair, etc.) without touching the ball. If the ball touches a player, that player goes to the penalty box. No goalies are used. Two balls at once can make the game even more exciting. *David Parke*

GAMES

Pool parties, lake retreats—if you're near a body of water, we've got contests and activities for you. Some involve boats and canoes; others require nothing more than a ball or a flotation device. If your kids are competent swimmers, they'll enjoy these games.

AQUATIC BASEBALL

This swimming pool game can be a lot of fun without being too hectic. You will need a rubber ball, or volleyball, and a medium-sized pool. Divide the group into two equal teams. The team that is up sits along the side and provides the pitcher. The players on other team are distributed throughout the pool (see diagram).

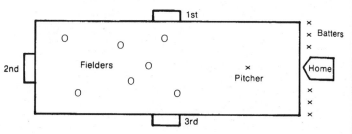

The batter gets only one pitch and must hit the ball with his or her hand. Anywhere inside the pool is a fair ball. The batter must then swim to the bases using any course he chooses to avoid an out. Outs are counted if the ball goes out of the pool, if the ball is caught in the air, if the player is tagged with the ball before reaching the base, or if the ball is thrown to first base before he reaches it. The other rules are the same as regular baseball—or you may agree to some additional rules of your own.

Or make these changes:
• Play with a whiffleball and bat.
• Play with two bases plus home plate (diving board).

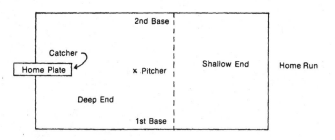

• Each team has four infielders (pitcher, first and second basemen, and catcher). Everyone else on the team is in the field (shallow water). The catcher, by the way, should be a good swimmer.

Russell Saito and Tom Bougher

CRAZY CANOE

Two people get in a canoe facing each other. Each has a paddle. One paddles one direction, the other paddles the other way. The winner is the one who can paddle the canoe across his goal line about 20 feet away. It is very difficult and hilarious to watch. The canoe tends to just go around in circles. This can be done in a large swimming pool. In a larger canoe, four or six people can play, with the two teams on each end of the canoe. *Tom Barwick*

DING BALL

This game is played in a swimming pool with a volleyball net dividing two teams. The teams are given every possible kind of ball (Ping-Pong, volley, football, soccer, beach ball, etc.). The object is to throw as many balls as possible over the net so that the opposing team has the most balls on their side when the whistle blows.

FLOATING ROCKS

Here is a challenging game that can be used in a swimming pool or in a lake, to take a break from the heavy splashing and frantic swimming. Have each person find a flat, smooth rock and bring it back to the water. Then tell each person to get in a floating position and place the flat rock on his or her forehead. Each person must float as long as possible with the rock on her forehead without bumping into someone or allowing the rock to fall off. Have an official, or the audience, time players by counting out seconds. Whoever lasts the longest is the winner. *Mary Kent*

GOLDFISH CHASE

Release a dozen small goldfish into a swimming pool (don't get big ones or fish from a backyard pond, they are very lazy). Team points are allowed for each one caught by hand. For added fun make players swim with clothes on. *Ralph Moore*

ICEBERG RELAY

Players push or pull a 25-pound block of ice to the opposite end of a swimming pool and back. It's frigid. Use several blocks of ice and award prizes for the best time. *Ralph Moore*

IN AND OUT RACE

This game is for use in shallow lake water. Race several canoes or rowboats at one time (three to five people per boat). Mark a finish line with bobbing markers about 50 feet from the starting line. Boaters are to propel themselves to the finish line without using oars, just hands. Whenever the leader blows the whistle, players must get out of the boat, jump back in, then paddle on. The leader should blow the whistle often. The first team to cross the finish line wins.

JUMP OR DIVE

This old favorite requires midair decision making. One at a time the young people take a nice, high bounce off the diving board. At the height of their jump, you yell either "Jump!" or "Dive!"—and the young person must obey. You'll see some wild contortions as kids try to change their water-entry positions in a split second. If a hand hits the water first, it's ruled a dive; if a foot hits first, a jump.

If the kids get too good at second-guessing you, wait longer before you yell your command. Or really tie them in knots with an occasional "Jive!" *John Yarnell*

SHARK IN THE DARK

This is the west version of American Eagle (page 49). The object is for swimmers to swim through the shark-infested waters without being attacked.

The swimming area has two safety points 20 feet apart. Appoint one of your youths to be the shark. The shark waits near one end of the swimming area, and all of the swimmers are at the other end. At a given signal, the shark submerges and all of the swimmers make for the opposite safety area. The shark must travel and make all attacks while swimming under water. The shark must bring his victim's shoulders out of the water to constitute a legal attack. Sharks may surface for visual sightings of their victims and air as often as needed.

All of the swimmers who were attacked now become sharks for the next round. It is important to pause a moment so your sharks and swimmers can position themselves before you signal the next round to begin. This allows time for the sharks to rest and plan their strategy.

As the game progresses you should have more sharks and fewer swimmers. The last swimmer attacked is the winner. The first one attacked becomes the shark for the next game. The game works best in a lake in four to five feet of water, although a pool is satisfactory. *Gary Ogdon*

STRIPPER RELAY

Give each team an identical set of baggy clothing (shirts with buttons, pants with zippers, etc.). Place the clothes in individual team piles about 20 yards from the starting line on a raft or at the end of a pool. At the starting signal, one member of each team swims to the raft or end of the pool, climbs out of the water, puts the clothes on, strips the clothes off, and swims back to his team. He touches the next member of the team who then swims through the same process. First team to finish the process wins.

• **Sweatshirt Relay.** Or try it this way. The object is to run through the water to a predetermined point and back, give the sweatshirt to the next contestant, and sit down. Obviously, if the sweatshirt is not changed correctly, the contestants may be there all day. The best way to get the sweatshirt from one person to the other is to have both contestants lean toward each other and hold hands with arms outstretched. The sweatshirt can then be pulled off of one and onto the other easily by another teammate. (Contestants must have the sweatshirt completely on before running into water.)

SUMMER SNOWMAN

Next time you're at the river or lake or ocean, take along a can or two of spray snow, some scarves, hats,

and other cold-weather clothing. Your kids will have a great time building a sandman, spraying it with canned snow, then dressing it. If you really want to get people's attention, you can stand around your summer snowmen in your swimsuits and sing Christmas carols. *Ian Mayhew*

SURFBOARD RELAY

Players line up and paddle to the opposite end of the pool and back while seated or lying backward on surfboards. Paddling backward is ridiculous and awkward, so everyone gets a huge laugh as well as a good game. *Ralph Moore*

TAXI

This swimming pool game begins with two teams, each with an air mattress, on opposite sides of the pool. On "Go!" one member of each team straddles his mattress and paddles it around the pool. When the two players arrive back at their own starting points, they each pick up another teammate and make another lap—and this continues until the entire team is on the mattress.

The trick is mounting the mattress, especially with several kids already on it. There'll be a lot of thrashing and sputtering during this game! *Mark Ziehr*

WATER BRONCO

Tie a long rope to a "snow saucer," or any other flat-bottomed object you can ride on with a handle of some kind attached to it. Next, get several kids on the end of the rope (out of the water) and one person to ride the saucer while it is being pulled by the group across the pool or lake. The object is for the rider to hang on. It's a lot like water skiing. Teams can compete for best time, or you can do it just for fun. *Paul Mason*

WATER CARNIVAL

Next time you have a pool party, try some of these games:
• **Walk the Plank.** Tie a long narrow pole onto the diving board so that it extends out over the

water. Mark it off at one foot intervals. See who can walk out on it the farthest. The markings on the pole indicate how far each person gets.

• **Submarine Races.** See who can swim the farthest underwater.

• **Ugly Dive Contest.** See who can complete the most unusual dive.

• **Cannonball.** See who can make the biggest splash off the board.

• **Pearl Diving Contest.** Kids dive for coins thrown into the pool. The team with the most money wins.

• **Potato Race.** This is done in shallow water, but can be done in deep water if your kids are good swimmers. Kids carry a potato on a spoon to a goal and back, relay style. If the potato falls off, it must be picked up with the spoon. They cannot touch the potato with their hands.

• **Boat Tug-of-War.** Two boats are needed. Simply tie a rope between the two boats, place them in the center of the lake or racing area, and at the signal, the players in each boat try to reach their goal on opposite ends of the lake or pool. In other words, it's a tug-of-war with boats. More than one

boat can go on each end of the rope (end to end) if you have enough boats and room.

WATER AND WATER BALLOON GAMES

Who says you need a pool or lake to enjoy liquid fun? These games are the ticket to refresh your kids on a hot summer day. Whether the games involve water balloons or Super Soakers, your group is guaranteed a sopping good time.

RUN 'N' WET

Have your kids sit in a circle and number themselves off, then put a plump water balloon in the center of the circle. When the leader calls out two numbers, those two kids must jump up and run around the circle back to their own place—but no stopping yet. They must race through the empty spot they left to the water balloon in the middle.

Can you guess the rest? Yup—first one there gets to throw the balloon at the loser, who must stand still and not dodge it. *Lisa Nyman*

CANDLE DRAW

Divide a large outdoor area (or an indoor area you can get wet) into five pie-shaped sections. Place five candles across a tabletop located at the back of each area. Position one player in each section with a loaded Super Soaker water gun. Light the candles and give a signal for the play to begin.

Players defend their own candles at the same time they attempt to douse the others. The winning player is the one with the most lit candles when the water supply runs out.

Adapt this game any of a number of ways, depending on the makeup of your group and the availability of supplies:
- Use a smaller or larger number of sections.
- Create a tournament and award points.
- Organize two-player, two-soaker teams, or larger teams with a limited number of guns.
- Place buckets of water in the playing areas; the winner is the one with the last candle still flickering.
- Place the water supply outside of the sections so participants have to leave their candles unguarded while they are getting refills.

Len Cuthbert

DESPERATION

Two teams get on opposite sides of the room, each staying behind a line. For each round, one person from each team is blindfolded. A squirt gun is then placed somewhere in the middle between the two teams. The two blindfolded players try to find the squirt gun. Their teammates may help them by yelling out directions. As soon as one of the players finds the squirt gun, they may remove their blindfold and go squirt the other player who is still blindfolded. The player who didn't find the squirt gun may try to run back to her team's line to avoid being squirted, but she may not remove her blindfold.

Points are scored as follows:

• Finding the squirt gun—50 points.

• Squirting the other player—50 points.

• Removing the blindfold illegally—(before the squirt gun is found or while you are being pursued by the person with the squirt gun)—minus 100 points.

This game can also be played outdoors on a warm day using water balloons. *Gary Sumner*

FLAMINGOS

This game works best outdoors with two contestants at a time. The winners can compete in play-offs until there is a champion. Each player is given a filled water pistol. Players must hold one foot off of the ground and hop while squirting other players, making them lose their balance. The round is over when someone drops his other foot to the ground, or when both contestants are out of water. In the event neither person loses his balance, a judge determines the winner based on who is the driest. *Kathie Taylor*

WATER BAGGIES

The water balloon is an indispensable ingredient in youth ministry games. But how many hours do youth leaders spend filling balloons for the group?

One alternative is to have buckets of water ready and a supply of plastic sandwich bags, of the fold-lock top variety. As the game gets underway, the participants fill the bags by holding them under water and closing the top. The result is an instant, very temporary, water balloon substitute. Another advantage is that cleanup is easier than with regular water balloons. *Tim Gerarden*

LEMON SHOOT OUT

Save up plastic lemons that contain lemon or lime juice. These lemons make great squirt guns. Line up participants of the game into two lines facing each other approximately 10 feet apart, equipping each person with a lit candle and a water-filled plastic lemon. Have each person put the lit candle in front of his face. On "Go," all participants try to extinguish all the candle flames of the opposing team. First team to extinguish all the other team's candles wins. This game can also be played with squirt guns. *Grant Lee*

POP BOTTLE FIRING SQUAD

Players score points by knocking plastic pop bottles off a board with water guns. To set up the game, place two chairs back-to-back, six to eight feet apart. Place a board on the backs of the chairs and two-liter plastic pop bottles on top of the board. Collect two or more pump-action water guns. Play and scoring may be by individuals or teams.

Set players, loaded water guns in hand, on opposite sides of the board. The players shoot from a distance to knock the bottles off the board onto the

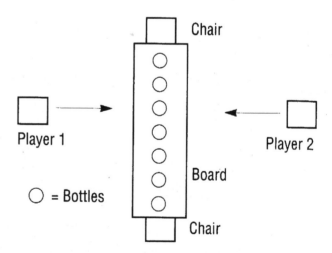

other side. Of course, players will also get wet during the battle. When all the bottles are knocked off, the game is over. The winner can be determined by the number of bottles each side knocks off or by the number of bottles on each side of the board.

The pop bottles can also be marked with point values to vary the competition. *Len Cuthbert*

Shoot the Duck

This game can be played with any size group from six to 60. The leader has everyone assemble in one large circle, with all the participants facing in the same direction. Each one in the circle puts his hand on the shoulder of the person ahead of him. Several leaders or young people, depending on the size of the group, stand at various spots within the circle facing those in the circle, armed with loaded squirt guns.

At a given signal, the leader has the whole group rotate in a circle while music is being played (or until a whistle is blown). When the music stops, the person immediately in front of each of the armed leaders is shot with the squirt gun just like a sitting duck. The ones who have been shot must leave the game. The circle then closes up and the music begins again. The circle again moves around until the music stops and the ducks are shot. This procedure continues until only one is left. The last one to stay in the game is declared the winner. (As more and more participants leave the game, the leader might want to decrease the number of shooters.) This game is exciting and the tension runs high. *Samuel Hoyt*

Laser Squirt

To get the same effect produced by expensive laser-tag guns, try this version of tag. Use water-color markers to color a three-inch circle on a 4x6-inch card for each participant. Ask kids to bring their

squirt guns and wear old shirts; you provide buckets for refilling. Tape a card to the chest of each player—and have at it! When the colored circle is hit with water, the color runs—and that player is dead and out of the game.

Form five-person color-coded teams and allow a few minutes of pregame planning before signaling hostilities to commence. The team with the most unsquirted members at the end of the time period wins. *Mark Adams*

Fizzer Tag

Before you play this summertime, Laser Tag-type outdoor game, drill a small hole in the center of as many Alka-Seltzer tablets as you have kids, and then run a string through each tablet in order to hang it loosely around a player's neck. Have each player bring a squirt gun, provide several full buckets of water out-of-bounds for refills, and begin the game.

The object? When a player's Alka-Seltzer tablet gets hit enough and dissolves sufficiently to drop off the string, that player is out. To shorten the game, bring out the garden hose! *Jeff Minor*

Fizzer War

Fizzer War has complex objectives that makes this a fun, challenging team game.

Preparing for war: At each end of a large field set up—
• A waterproof chair
• Three buckets marked FOOTBALLS, FRISBEES, and TENNIS BALLS
• A "safe base" where players are immune to enemy fire, so they can rest and reload.

Mark your playing field like this:

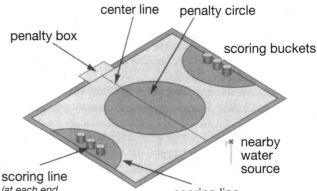

center line   penalty circle

penalty box

scoring buckets

scoring line
*(at each end,
one bucket for footballs,
one bucket for frisbees,
one bucket for tennis balls)*

nearby water source

scoring line
*(players cannot get any
closer than this line to the
buckets—about 10' out)*

Create a large supply of fizzer medallions: Drill a small hole in the center of each Alka-Seltzer tablet, thread 24-inch strings through the holes, and tie the ends together so kids can slip them over their heads. Make enough for one per player per round.

Collect footballs, Frisbees, and tennis balls for offensive play. Collect water balloons, Super Soakers, buckets, or cups (or a combination of these) for defensive play. The amount of each that you will need depends on the size of your group; plan on having plenty on hand. Be sure you have a source of water handy. Have copies of the score sheet (page 125) and pencils available.

Waging war: The objective of Fizzer War is to score the most points by landing the balls and Frisbees in the appropriately labeled buckets. No points are awarded for the wrong bucket or for near misses. Players must be wearing an Alka-Seltzer medallion to participate, so teens can eliminate opponents by getting the Alka-Seltzer wet—eventually causing it to fall off. Once a tablet dissolves enough to drop off the string, that player sits out for the rest of the round.

One person from each team must sit in the chair near the team's base for each round—a "sitting duck" of sorts. Points are scored for each water hit on this person, and bonus points are awarded if the sitting duck's Alka-Seltzer falls off.

Before play begins, let each team meet for a few minutes to pick a team name; develop strategies; and select a water-balloon filler, a "sitting duck," and a scorekeeper. They also may want to choose a goalkeeper-type person to recover footballs, Frisbees, and tennis balls and throw them far down field.

Play six rounds of seven to 10 minutes each, with 10-minute rest periods between rounds. Players can come and go freely to the safe base, where they can't play or be hit. They can travel the entire field, but not across the field line 10 feet away from the scoring buckets.

Ground rules:
• Throw only water at other players.
• No hits above the shoulders.
• No one can cover his Alka-Seltzer.
• No holding onto anyone.

The penalty for violating any of these rules? Into the penalty circle for five seconds, where one is unprotected from a water assault!

Want to encourage more teamwork, strategy, and scoring? Limit the water supply—say, one five-gallon bucket per round. *Dave Mahoney*

FIREFIGHTER WATER WARS

Add this to your list of outdoor, hot-weather water games. You'll need the cooperation of your local fire department, because the game requires a garden-hose adapter to a fire hydrant (fire departments have them). Or hook up your hoses to your normal water spigots if the water pressure is sufficient for this game.

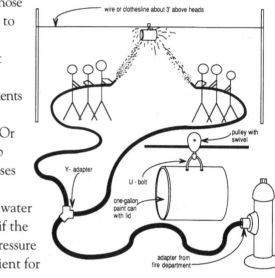

Use the adapter to hook up three hoses (see diagram), and suspend an empty paint can on a pulley hanging from a wire or clothesline. Two teams will each use the water stream from their hoses to move an empty paint can toward the opposing team's end. Of course, both teams will have an immensely fun and soaking time of it. Form teams and conduct a tournament. *Bev Illian*

WATERLOGGED VOLLEYBALL

Put a pole in the middle of the volleyball net with a

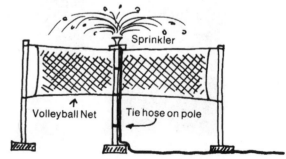

sprinkler at the top and the hose hooked to the pole. Then just play a regular game of volleyball. If

Fizzer War
SCORE SHEET

Team Name _____

Period One

_____ footballs x 1000 points = _____

_____ Frisbees x 1000 points = _____

_____ tennis balls x 1000 points = _____

_____ chair target hits x 1000 points = _____

1 chair target bonus x 5000 points = _____

TOTAL points for period one = _____

Period Two

_____ footballs x 2000 points = _____

_____ Frisbees x 2000 points = _____

_____ tennis balls x 2000 points = _____

_____ chair target hits x 2000 points = _____

1 chair target bonus x 10,000 points = _____

TOTAL points for period two = _____

Period Three

_____ footballs x 5000 points = _____

_____ Frisbees x 5000 points = _____

_____ tennis balls x 5000 points = _____

_____ chair target hits x 5000 points = _____

1 chair target bonus x 15,000 points = _____

TOTAL points for period three = _____

Period Four

_____ footballs x 8000 points = _____

_____ Frisbees x 8000 points = _____

_____ tennis balls x 8000 points = _____

_____ chair target hits x 8000 points = _____

1 chair target bonus x 20,000 points = _____

TOTAL points for period four = _____

Period Five

_____ footballs x 10,000 points = _____

_____ Frisbees x 10,000 points = _____

_____ tennis balls x 10,000 points = _____

_____ chair target hits x 10,000 points = _____

1 chair target bonus x 25,000 points = _____

TOTAL points for period five = _____

Period Six

_____ footballs x 15,000 points = _____

_____ Frisbees x 15,000 points = _____

_____ tennis balls x 15,000 points = _____

_____ chair target hits x 15,000 points = _____

1 chair target bonus x 30,000 points = _____

TOTAL points for period six = _____

Game Total: _____

you are playing on the grass, be aware of the possible damage that will occur to the grass. This game would best be played on a dirt surface that will get nice and muddy. *Nick Tomeo*

PIKE'S PEAK

Create two teams and have each team choose a captain. Both captains are stranded on Pike's Peak, which is located 200 to 300 yards from Pike's Dam (a water source such as a huge bucket or garbage can filled with water). Each captain holds an empty gallon container. Each team member is given a small paper or plastic cup. The object is to fill the cup with water at Pike's Dam (the only water source allowed) and to fill the captain's container. The first team to have a full container wins. Opponents are allowed to try to stop the other team by spilling their water in the small cups or by throwing water all over them.

Rules:
• Guys cannot attack girls.
• Girls can attack guys.
• Within two feet of the captain is a "free zone." No combat can take place there.
• Distinguish teams by placing colorful tape on player's foreheads.

PONY EXPRESS

This is an outdoor game that requires a paved area, bicycles, stepladders, and the use of water. It's a great game for a warm, sunny day.

Divide into teams of any number, depending on how many bicycles and ladders you have. Form a circular track, with ladders lining the inside of the track (see diagram). Each ladder has a bucket of water on it and a paper cup.

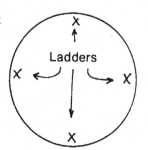

Bike riders are equipped with containers tied to their heads. You can take an old straw hat, turn it upside down, and cut slits through it. Then place a scarf through the slits and tie it under the chin. Line the inside of the hat with plastic and place a plastic bowl inside the hat. The straw-hat shaped containers that potted plants come in are perfect. The illustration below might help!

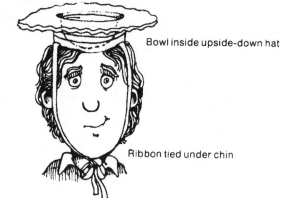

Bowl inside upside-down hat

Ribbon tied under chin

Riders then get on the bicycles (with their hats on) and ride around in the circle as close to the ladders as possible. Teammates are stationed on the ladders, and they try to toss water in the hats of the riders as they ride by. After each lap, the riders dump off their water into a container and continue until the time limit is up (five minutes is usually sufficient, but it could be longer). Each team goes separately and the team that collects the most water within the time limit is the winner.

If the procedure seems too complicated, try playing this game with your own set-up. For example, the bike riders could carry water containers on baskets attached to the handlebars, or they could be pulling wagons with buckets in them, or whatever. Use your imagination. You could substitute tricycles for bicycles, or just have the students run around the circle instead of using bikes. The possibilities are endless. *Brenda Clowers*

SABOTAGE WATER WAR

Give each player a large plastic cup full of water and have them spread out over an area the size of a basketball court. They hold their cups in their left hands and try to upset other players' cups with their right hands. They cannot throw the water at anyone, they only try to knock the water out of each other's cups. The last one to remain on the court with some water in his cup wins. *David Coppedge*

SPONGE DODGE

In the heat of the summer, find a beach or open lawn, take along four or five five-gallon buckets and an equal number of sponges, and cool yourselves off with this game.

Mark out a circle and place the buckets around the perimeter. Half fill them with water, and drop a sponge or two in each. After the entire youth group gets in the circle, the leader soaks the first sponge and throws (aim below the head). Those who get hit join the leader around the edge, and the game continues until only one is left—the winner. Sponges that drop inside the circle can be retrieved by any thrower, but they must be dipped again before they are thrown.

Some variations:
• Reverse the game. That is, when someone is hit, the thrower joins those inside the circle. Last one on the perimeter loses.
• Play by teams. Time how long it takes for one team to get all members of an opposing team hit and out of the circle. Shortest time wins. Or set a time limit—the winning team has the most members still in the circle when the clock runs out.
• Run the game indefinitely, with no winners or losers. Begin the game with five inside the circle. Whoever makes a hit trades places with his victim.

Vernal Wilkinson

WATERBALL SAMURAI

The object of this wet warfare is to hit the other team's samurai with a water-soaked foam ball as many times as possible in one minute.

You will need a whiffle bat, foam balls (at least six), water buckets (at least three), a step stool (from the water fountain), time keeper and point counter, chalk or tape.

Make boundaries for the game by drawing or marking with tape a six-foot-diameter circle. Place the low stool in the center of the circle. Place three buckets on a line, 15 feet outside the circle's edge,

Divide the groups into teams of five or six players each, and ask each team to select one player to be the samurai. The samurai from the defending team stands on the stool in the center of the circle and may not step off the stool during the round. The remaining

defending team members position themselves on the perimeter of the circle to defend their samurai from the waterballs. They can not move into the circle or beyond its perimeter. They must confine their movements to the edge of the circle. Their samurai, meanwhile, defends himself with a Whiffle bat to divert waterballs.

From behind the water-bucket line, the opposing team throws water-soaked foam balls at the samurai in the circle, attempting to hit him. If a thrown ball falls short of the circle, an offensive team member may run up to retrieve it and either carry it back to the line to throw it again or else toss it to one of the other team members already behind the line, who may then throw the ball at the samurai. Offensive players may not, however, enter the defending team's circle to retrieve any balls.

The round ends when one minute is up or all the waterballs are inside the circle. The offensive team gets one point each time they hit the samurai with a waterball or for each time the samurai steps off the step stool.

If you have more than three or four teams, you may want to get more foam balls and mark out more waterball courts so you can have several games going on simultaneously. Winners from each court can play one another in a championship game.

Doug Partin

WET SPONGE

This is a fun get-acquainted game that works best with a group of at least 30. Have the group make a fairly large circle (about an arm's length from each other). In the center, place a large bucket of water. Have about five people start out as "It" (in a camp situation, have the staff start as "It"). Each person who is "It" gets a sponge soaked with water and runs up to a different person in the circle and says,"Wet Sponge," and that person answers "Take a plunge," which is responded to with, "Who's a grunge?" and the person in the circle names another person in the circle. The person with the sponge then runs up to that person and hits them with the soaked sponge. That person is now "It." The game goes very rapidly and ends when everyone is soaked or the water is gone. *The camp staff of Susquehanna Valley Presbytery and Susquehanna Association of the U.C.C.*

WET 'N' WILD BASEBALL

Play this game in a park with whatever baseball rules you like. Make the competition unique by using 30 gallon kiddie pools or garbage cans filled with water for bases and a Slip'n'Slide to get to home plate. Let kids know in advance to come dressed in swimsuits or shorts and T-shirts. You will also need a garden hose and access to a water faucet.

Use a large plastic bat and rubber ball. After hitting the ball, players place both legs in the water-filled garbage cans as they go around. To score they must run down the third-base line and slide into home using the Slip'n'Slide. Teams may have multiple runners on a base. It's lively when several people try to slide home together.

Variation: Use a water sprinkler for first base or for all bases. *Drew Hulse and Michael W. Capps*

MISSILE MANIA

For a massive-strike water-balloon fight, purchase two water-balloon slingshots and mark off a playing field (see diagram). At each end of the field is a launching pad where several designated players work the slingshot. In between the pads is a hand-to-hand open combat zone (the OCZ) where individuals may hand-throw water balloons at opponents. A player hit with a water balloon must go to the opposition's prison, located near the launching pad. There's also a safety zone at each end in which a player is immune from being taken prisoner and into which no opposition players may enter.

The object of the game is to hit a launcher on the opposition with a water balloon, thereby knocking out their launching pad.

After you divide the group into two teams, each team designates players who must remain at all times in their team's launching pad and use the water-balloon launcher to fire balloons over the OCZ in an attempt to hit any of the enemy launchers. Once a launcher is hit by a balloon, the pad is considered "knocked out," and the opposing team scores a point.

Other players engage in hand-to-hand balloon combat in the OCZ as they try to knock out a launching pad by throwing the balloons. In addition, they try to take enemy prisoners by hitting them in the OCZ. Those hit in the OCZ must remain in the opposition's prison until a knockout point is scored by their own team, at which time they are freed and may join the war again.

The first team to score 10 knockout points wins. *Gene Stabe*

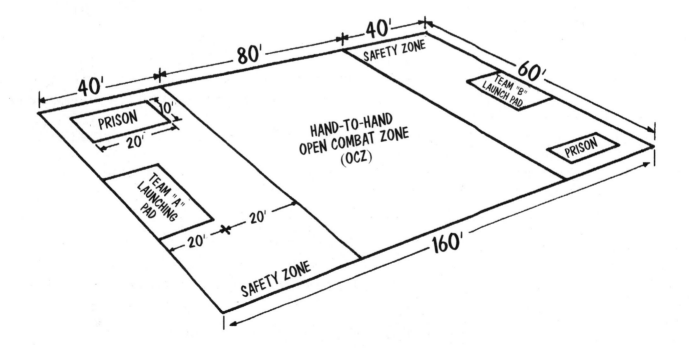

MUDDY MARBLE SCRAMBLE

Here's a wild game for hot weather and large groups. Churn up a mud hole (figure approximately one to two square feet per kid). Then work hundreds of different colored marbles into the top five or six inches of mud. (Make sure the mud doesn't have too many rocks.) Each different colored marble is worth a different amount of points. The fewer you have of one color, the more points they are worth. For example:

> 1 red marble: 500 points
> 2 white marbles: 100 points each
> 25 blue marbles: 50 points each
> 100 green marbles: 20 points each

Divide the group up into teams, each with two leaders—one who washes off the recovered marbles, the other keeps track of how many of each color have been recovered. At the signal, all of the participants dive in the mud and search for marbles for 10 to 15 minutes. When time is called, the team with the most points wins. *Ted Thisse*

MUDDY WATERS PILLOW FIGHT

This is a good game for camps. Individuals do battle seated on a 10-inch diameter pole suspended a few feet over a creek or mudhole. You can dig the puddle if you don't own one. The object is to knock the competition off the pole and into the water with a pillow. This is a team action with points going to the winner's side. Teams should be comprised of about 15 members. If the group is large enough, a tournament may be played. *Ralph Moore*

MUSICAL SQUIRT GUN

This exciting game can be played with a group ranging from six to 30, indoors or out. Have the group sit in a circle either on chairs or on the floor. A loaded squirt gun is passed around the circle until the music stops. The person who is holding the squirt gun at that time must leave the game. But before he leaves, he may squirt the person on his left or right twice or squirt both once. After his chair is removed, the circle moves in a bit and the game continues. The last person left is declared the winner.

The gun must be passed with two hands and received with two hands or else it will be frequently dropped and will break. Also, it works best to have a second loaded squirt gun on hand to be substituted for the one that becomes empty. An assistant can then refill the original gun while the second one is being used. Be sure to emphasize that only two squirts are allowed. Otherwise you will be continually refilling the squirt guns. This is an exciting game. As teens are eliminated they will be gunnin' for a particular person, and you will not be able to water down the excitement. *Samuel Hoyt*

MUSICAL WASHTUBS

Here's a refreshing game for hot summer days. First you will need to secure the use of several large washtubs—no small trick if you live in the suburbs. Then fill the tubs with water and arrange them in a circle. Now the game is just like musical chairs. You have one more person than you have washtubs, and while the music plays, everyone marches around the tubs. When the music stops (or a whistle is blown, etc.), each person must find a tub and sit in it—all the way. The person without a tub is eliminated. One tub is removed and the game continues until only one tub remains and two people must fight for it. The winner is whoever winds up in the last tub. As the game progresses, it will be necessary to have someone with a hose (or two) to keep the tubs full of water. A variation is to fill the tubs with mud. *Bob Messer*

VOLLEY-BALLOON WATERBALL

The crazy name is to avoid possible confusion of this game with Water Balloon Volleyball. To play this unique game, you will need a regular volleyball net, lots of filled water balloons, and two king-sized sheets or blankets.

There are two teams, one on each side of the net. Each team gets a sheet and the entire team surrounds the sheet, holding it by the edges. A water balloon is placed in the middle of the serving team's sheet, and the team must lob the balloon over the net using the sheet like a trampoline.

The other team must try to catch the balloon on its sheet (without causing it to break) and then heave it back over the net to the opposing team. If it goes out of bounds or lands back in their side of the court, they lose the point or serve. If the receiving team fails to catch it, or if it breaks in-bounds, then they lose.

The scoring is the same as in regular volleyball. Teams can be any size, but if you get too many people around the sheets, it becomes difficult to move quickly. The game requires great teamwork and is perfect for a hot day. *Dan Sarian*

WATER BALLOON BLITZ

Make sure everyone has brought a change of clothes before you begin playing this game. Create teams and give a bunch of deflated balloons to each team (about four or fiver per player). Each team has 15 minutes to fill balloons with water (provide a separate spigot for each team). Then let players go crazy with a blitz until there are no more water balloons left. The driest team wins.

WATER BALLOON BOPPERS

Here's a new way to have a water balloon war. Have everyone bring a regular sock to use—long tube socks work best. Then give each person a water balloon, which goes inside the sock.

Now have a water balloon fight in which kids try to tag each other with their water balloon boppers. Hits must be below the shoulders. If your water balloon breaks, you are out of the game, but if

you can hit someone without breaking your water balloon, then you can remain in the game to hit someone else. The winner is the last person left with a water balloon still intact.

A variation of this game would be to eliminate anyone who gets tagged as well as anyone whose water balloon breaks. Either way, it's lots of fun. *Jim Ruberg*

WATER BALLOON CATAPULT

This has to be one of the most exciting and fun game ideas you'll ever use. Punch two holes in a half football and slide on to the center of a long piece of surgical tubing. Tie the tubing to two stakes. Place

water balloons in the half football, pull back, and let her fly. You should be able to lob balloons up to 40 yards without any trouble. Of course, you can have two teams face each other in battle or try to lob the balloons directly at certain targets.

Caution: This can be dangerous and destructive. If balloons are lobbed low or at close range, they can dent a car or break windows and people's heads. *Dave Anderson*

WATER BALLOON DODGE

This game is exactly like dodgeball except, of course, you use water balloons. Line one team up against the wall and the other team a minimum of 20 feet back. The last person to get hit by a water balloon wins. *Tim Lawrence*

WATER BALLOON RELAY

Have pairs of kids race between two points holding a water balloon between their foreheads. No hands allowed. If the balloon drops, the pair takes 10 steps back, then starts running toward the goal again. If the balloon breaks, the pair is out of the game.

WATER BALLOON SHOT PUT

See who can toss a water balloon shot put-style the farthest. To make the game more interesting, have a leader stand in an area that will make him a likely target.

WATER BALLOON SOCCER

Divide the group into as many teams of 10 to 15 as you can. Before the game, fill a minimum of three water balloons per team member. Also prepare one hat (or helmet) per team: With duct tape, affix tacks, point out, to a helmet or ball cap. The hat is then placed on an X on the ground about 20 feet from the starting line.

At a signal, the first person in line for each team runs to the hat and puts it on. The second person in the line lobs a balloon in the air in the general direction of the first player, who attempts to break the balloon with the hat. If the hat-wearing teammate misses, a second and third balloon are thrown. If he still doesn't puncture a balloon with his hat (and drench himself in the process), he puts the hat down and goes to the end of his line—and the next teammate in line tries her luck. The first team that cycles the entire team through wins the event. *Brad Edgbert*

WATER BALLOON VOLLEYBALL

Water Balloon Volleyball is played very similarly to a regular game of conventional volleyball. Set up your volleyball net as usual, and divide the young people into equal teams. Any number of young people may play. The main difference in this game is that instead of using a regular volleyball, you use a water balloon that is caught and tossed.

The service takes place from the back line and each team is allowed three tosses and three catches in order to get the water balloon over the net to the opposing team. The opposing team then has three tosses and three catches in order to get the ball back across the net. The balloon is continually tossed back and forth across the net until, finally, breakage occurs. When the balloon breaks, the side on which it breaks does not score, but rather the opposite team gets the point, without regard to who did the serving.

Spikes are allowed, but again, if the balloon breaks on the team who is doing the spiking, the other team is awarded the point. The team that wins the point, regardless of which team it is, is the team that continues to serve until service is broken.

The game is played to a regular volleyball score of 15, at which time sides of the net are changed and the game resumes. All other rules in regular volleyball are in effect for this game, such as out-of-bound lines, not being able to cross over the net with your hand, or falling into the net with your body.

Another variation of this game which proves to be even more fun is to have 30 or 40 members on each team and insert into play four or five water balloons, so that there are several opportunities for returns, spikes, and services all at the same time. The rules for this game are the same as for the one-ball system. There is no official scoring for this game. The winning team is simply the driest team at the end of an allotted period of time. *Terry McIlvain*

BLIND WATER BALLOON VOLLEYBALL

You need a good supply of water balloons and a volleyball net draped with blankets so that opposing teams can't see each other.

The first team serves a water balloon by tossing it underhand over the net (as opposed to throwing it hard and fast).

It might also be a good idea to run a line above the net (approximately 15 feet high) and require that the players throw the balloons over that line to avoid spikes and line drives. *Elene Harge*

WATER BALLOON WAR

This game is similar to Wells Fargo (page 151) or other camp games that involve the use of a large area and lots of kids. Divide into two teams and somehow mark players with an identifying color (such as arm bands, badges, etc.). Each team has a target (a person) that remains in one spot during the game, and the object of the game is simply to hit the other team's target person with a water balloon. Each team prepares ahead of time a large number of water balloons (about six times more than the number of players on the team) and keeps them at the team's home base. No player may enter another team's home base to destroy their arsenal of balloons.

As the game starts, players on both teams get two balloons each and try to reach the target person of the other team. Opposing team members may kill each other by hitting the other team members with water balloons. Dead players must leave the game. The first team to hit the target wins, and the game either ends or goes into round two. Scoring may be kept by awarding 100 points for every kill made and 500 points may be awarded for hitting the target. *Jerry Martin*

WATER BALLOON WHOMPIES

Each team member gets three to five water balloons. Draw a circle on the ground and one entire team sits down inside the circle, while another team lobs water balloons at them. The sitting team cannot move. The throwing team must stay behind a given line. They are required to throw the balloons underhanded and on a 10-foot arc. Anybody breaking the rules must sit down on a full water balloon. The teams trade places when one team runs out of balloons. Give a prize to the driest team. *Steve Tidwell*

BOMBS AWAY

For this game you will need to make a five-to six-foot tall partition out of cardboard or plywood (or whatever you have handy). It should also be about five or six feet wide with a 10-inch diameter hole somewhere near the top. The partition can be free standing, or you can have two people hold it up while the game is being played.

Divide your group into teams. One person from each team lies down on the floor facing up with his feet toward the partition (under the hole). The rest of the team lines up on the other side of the partition, water balloons in hand. The object of the game is for players to kneel down on a "tossing line," and toss the water balloon through the hole so that the person lying down on the other side can catch it before it breaks. No warning or signal can be given before tossing the water balloon. The team that has the most unbroken water balloons after every person has tossed (or at the end of a time limit) is the winner. It's a messy game that can be a lot of fun.

Substitute raw eggs for a gooier version. *Brenda Clowers*

BUSTED

Every group has at least some kids who would burst water balloons over their heads if they knew that a five dollar bill was in one of the balloons. So on a hot day, give your group a hilarious show, make someone five dollars richer—and maybe pull an object lesson from the silliness (what people will do for money, paying a price for getting what one really wants, etc.). Give volunteers only seven seconds; let more volunteers try their luck until the money is found. *Timothy Bean*

FLING 'EM

Divide lots of water balloons equally between four teams, and send each team to one of the corners in the playing area (see diagram).

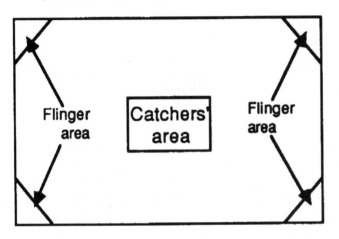

Each team selects two people to be its catchers, who take a garbage can with them into the catchers' area. When the game begins, teams attempt to lob (no line drives) their water balloons from their corners to their own catchers' garbage can in the middle of the playing area. The team with the most water in their can when all balloons are gone wins.

Remember these rules:
- Both catchers must hold the garbage can.
- Catchers can catch balloons from any team.
- No physical contact between opposing catchers is permitted unless they're vying for tossed balloons.
- Catchers cannot step out of their designated area.

Devise various ways of propelling the balloons to the cans: slingshots made from surgical tubing (make sure balloons are lobbed high into the air, not directed at the catchers), plastic throwers shaped like those used in Jai Alai, etc. *John Stumbo*

KAMIKAZE

This is an outdoor game, good for camps or with any group of 30 or more kids. Divide the group into two teams. One team will be identified by blue and the other by gold. These colors can be made with arm bands. Each team has a president who can only be assassinated by a water balloon. The playing area should be divided in half, with each team's president located in its own half of the total playing area. The president is seated in a chair that is inside a four-foot circle, which is in the center of a larger circle, some 30 or 40 feet in diameter.

Each team has the same set-up for their own president in separate locations. Both teams have offensive and defensive players. The offensive players each get two water balloons and may move in any part of the boundaries except for the area that composes the two circles with the presidents in the center. No person (offensive or defensive) may enter or pass through the two circles that surround

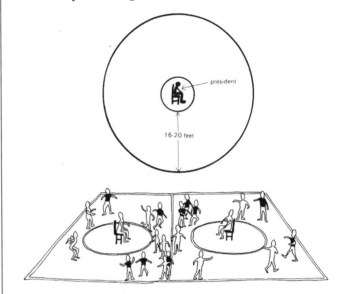

the presidents.

The offensive players try to assassinate the president of the opposite team. He does this by tossing underhanded a water bomb (balloon) from the edge of the outer circle. The toss must have an arch in it. If the balloon hits below the waist of the president, he is merely wounded. It takes three wounds to assassinate him. A balloon hitting on target (above the waist) kills the president and the game is over (or if not over, points are scored and the team elects a new president). An adult judge should be on hand to determine the legality of shots.

Defensive players are armed with a small paper bag of flour. Obviously their job is to defend the president. They can kill the other team's offensive players by breaking the bag of flour on them. Offensive players cannot kill defensive players. They simply must run back into their own territory. Defensive players are not allowed into the other team's territory. When a defensive player kills an offensive player, he takes his arm band and the dead offensive player must go to the graveyard and is out of the game. When all of the offensive players of a team are killed, they automatically lose the game.

The game is over after a time limit or when the president is assassinated. However, to prevent the game from being over too soon, it might be best to simply call a time-out when the president is assassinated and the teams have five minutes or so to reorganize, elect a new president, get their dead players back in the game and then the game resumes. Also, during the break, scores are taken by the scorekeeper. Assassination of the president is worth 200 points and arm bands of enemy players who are killed are worth 50 points each. New water balloons and flour sacks are passed out during each break that follows a president's assassination.

There should be at least four adult judges. One judge each for the team play areas and one judge to watch each president. Another person should be on hand to pass out flour sacks and balloons. (If a player uses up his supply at any time, he can go and get more.) This ammo area is safe and no fighting can be done there. *Lewis E. Trotter*

SAVE QUEEN BERTHA

Here's a water-balloon strategy game for outdoors.

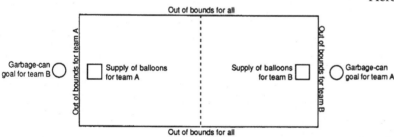

Set up a battlefield (see diagram) and provide each team with an equal number of three kinds of balloons:
• Red balloons (or another specified color) are worth 100 points.
• Queen Bertha balloons are very large (purchase at party-supply shops) and are worth 1,000 points. Only one per team.
• A variety of smaller balloons have no point value but are weapons.

Teams begin the game in their own territory, attempting to advance their point water balloons beyond enemy territory and score them into the garbage can. Weapon balloons are thrown at carriers of point balloons; those carrying point balloons who

get wet from an enemy's toss must relinquish their pointers to the enemy. This is the only way to steal points from the enemy—no physical contact or raiding of enemy supplies is permitted.

When about half the balloons are used, call a half-time so teams can reevaluate their strategies. When all the balloons are gone, the team with the most points in their garbage can wins. *John Stumbo*

SEARCH AND DESTROY

It's the last day of camp, the kids need an outdoor free-for-all, and—if you've been keeping track of team points all week—you need a final contest by which even the last-place team could conceivably catch up and win the entire week's competition.

So here's a combination scavenger hunt/water-balloon fight. First hide water balloons throughout the playing area (the more colors of balloons, the better). Begin the game itself by dividing players into teams and telling them the rules:
• After players find balloons, they must run, crawl, walk, sneak, or bluff their way back to "headquarters," where a sponsor tallies the balloons and records the score for the appropriate teams.
• Here's the twist: the point values of different balloon colors are not told to the players until the end of the game. (For example, yellow ones are 20 points each; blue, 15 points; red, 5 points; white, negative 5 points; pink, negative 10 points; three orange brought in on one trip by a player, 30 points; etc.).
• After the sponsor records players' points, the players are free to dispose of the balloons any way they want—and here's where the water-balloon fight begins.
• Players continue the process of finding, recording, and destroying until time runs out.

To keep the scorekeeper's skin dry, deduct big points for lobbing balloons at them. And when the melee is over, conduct a brief but crucial game to see which team can pick up the most balloon pieces. *David Holton*

A hot outdoor afternoon is perfect for this water-balloon game. One person throws a water balloon high in the air and calls out another player's name (or number, if the group has numbered off). The called player must catch the balloon. If she succeeds at catching it unbroken, she gets a free shot at the thrower who called her name and gets her turn at throwing a water balloon up and calling another's name.

If a water balloon breaks during an attempt to catch it—well, that player gets soaked. And if a called-out player doesn't even attempt to catch it, turn the hose on him! *Chris Hayes*

STRATEGIC CAPTURE THE FLAG

Water makes this version of Capture the Flag (page 49) a blast, and the strategic aspect makes your kids work together as a team.

All players tuck a sock, bandana, or rag into their waistbands. As in traditional Capture the Flag, players are captured when their sock is taken in enemy territory. Captured players are then imprisoned; you and the kids decide how and where.

Here are the twists that make Strategic Capture the Flag the high-powered game it is:

• **Safety zone.** Each team creates a safety zone—with a 10-foot circle of rope—around their flag. No one can be taken prisoner while inside this rope.

• **Gun emplacement.** Inside another 10-foot loop of rope, anywhere in the team's home turf, is a trash can full of water balloons. This is the team's gun emplacement—the only site from which water balloons may be thrown. Getting hit with a water balloon makes you a prisoner just like having your sock taken—except that such liquid shelling is effective anywhere, even on the enemy's own turf.

• **Tanks.** Each team also has two tanks—each one consists of two people, one riding piggyback on the other. The one on top has a plastic pitcher of water. Getting doused by a tank makes you a prisoner. Just remember two points: Tanks can take prisoners anywhere (on friendly or enemy territory), and only a tank can take another tank prisoner.

Make sure each team has a plentiful supply of water for their tanks, or have them agree on a neutral faucet. And use plenty of referees to avoid inventive rule bending.

Give each team plenty of prep time to make a strategy. You may want to play several shorter games instead of one long one; this gives each team a chance to try different strategies. *John Young*

SURPRISE MUSICAL CHAIRS

For this game, you will need chairs for everyone, some paper bags, and some balloons. Arrange the chairs for a regular game of musical chairs, only there should be enough chairs for everyone, rather than the usual one chair missing. Blow up balloons, put them inside the paper bags, close the bags, and place one on each chair. One of the sacks, however, contains a water balloon. The kids march around the chairs, and when the music stops (or on a signal) everyone sits down in a chair on top of the paper bag. Whoever gets the water balloon is out. Leaders can then reset the chairs with more bags, and so on, until the game gets down to one person left.

Obviously, this is going to take a lot of bags. If you would like to avoid that, have more (say, half) of the bags contain water balloons, and eliminate more kids the first time around. You can do the same with succeeding rounds also. Make sure the kids aren't watching while the chairs are being "armed." *J.R. Wallis*

ULTIMATE WATER BALLOONS

Played with a Frisbee, Ultimate Football (page 31) is a game that combines teamwork with athletic prowess as the Frisbee is moved down the field in nonstop, continuous play with any one of a number of various twists to the game.

A favorite warm-weather variation is to substitute water balloons for the Frisbee. The referee should be supplied with 36 water balloons in advance (for an approximately 30-minute game), which are stored up and down along the sidelines (this allows for quick replacement of the two balloons that the ref always carries in his hands). The referee must hustle to get a balloon to the other team when one breaks as soon as possible so that play is not unduly interrupted.

Kevin Turner

Giant Slip 'N' Slide Relay

With a 20-by-100-foot sheet of 6-mil plastic and a large, smooth grassy area, you're ready for fun! Spread out the plastic, hose it down, add some Johnson's Baby Shampoo to make it slick, and maybe some sprinklers along the sides to keep it wet.

Then start the relays: Team members must "swim" from end to end, be dragged by teammates (by hands or feet), or—the messiest of all—the watermelon relay. As racers run the course with a watermelon in their arms, adults pelt them with water balloons—as if the slippery plastic is not obstacle enough. When people drop their watermelons, they must pick up the pieces and continue the race.

When the free-for-all inevitably occurs, forbid the throwing of watermelon pieces (but not the stuffing of them in another's face). Free-for-all participants must stay on their knees. *Rick Brown*

Spit Relay

To play this outdoor relay, set up two large water jugs with spigots on opposite ends of a table, with the spigots hanging over the edge. Cut off the tops of a pair of two-liter soda bottles, and give one bottle to each team.

Players run to the water jug, fill their mouths from the spigot, run to the soda bottle, and spit the water into the team's bottle. The first team to overflow the bottle is the winner.

If you want to gross the kids out, take a drink from the winning team's bottle and throw the rest on the losing team.

Depending on the size of your group, you can vary the container so that each teen can go through the line two or three times. One two-liter bottle will hold about 30 to 40 mouthfuls.

For variation have players gargle the words, "Help! I'm sinking!" before spitting. *Brian Jennings*

Bottle Fill Relay

Give each team a small Styrofoam cup, an empty plastic soda bottle, and a bucket of water. One player from each team lies down on a goal line, places the empty soda bottle upright on her forehead, and holds it there. The other teammates line up along a starting line with the team bucket. The first player on each team fills the team's Styrofoam cup with water from the bucket, races to the team bottle, empties the water into the bottle, races back to the team, and hands off the cup to the next teammate in line. When the leader blows the whistle to end the game, the team with the most water in the soda bottle wins.

Double Duty Water Relay

For this relay each team needs a wastebasket-size container that will hold water reasonably well, a No. 10 tin can, a pop bottle, and a large supply of water (such as a barrel continuously replenished by a hose—anything that each team can fill their cans from without interfering with the other teams will do). This relay belongs outdoors, and kids should not wear good clothes.

Place a sturdy chair for each team about 50 feet away from the starting line, facing the line. Place each wastebasket on the line, its team lined up nearby, in pairs. One partner has the can filled with water, while the other carries the empty pop bottle. At the starting signal they run to the chair, one sits on the chair and holds the bottle upright on her head for her teammate to fill, using the can. (Don't let them bend the can.)

When the bottle is full or the can empty, whichever comes first, they run to the line and she empties the bottle into the wastebasket, while he refills the can and then both are given to the next pair. This pair takes its turn and so on to the end of the team. If the wastebasket isn't full yet, have the partners reverse roles. First team to overflow their basket wins. Works best with two large teams. *Rogers E. George III*

Waddle Walk Relay

Create teams of four people each. Two teammates line up at one line and face their teammates who are at the other line about 10 feet away. The first player on each team walks to the teammates at the other line while balancing a paper cup of water on his head and walking with an inflated balloon between his knees. If he reaches his other teammates successfully, he hands off the cup and balloon to the next person, who does the same and ends up at the other line. Any player who spills the water or drops the balloon must walk the distance again with the props until he is successful. The first team to have all four players successfully complete the relay wins.

FILL MY POCKETS RELAY

Divide into two or more teams. One guy puts a Coke bottle in his back pocket. The rest of the team lines up with dixie cups. The guy stands at one end of the line and a pail of water is at the other end. The idea is to transport the water, passing it from cup to cup, from the pail to the Coke bottle. The first group to do so wins. *Roger Copeland*

TYPHOON

Here is a relay game that is ideal for summer. Have two lines, single file, facing a water source. At a signal the first person in each line runs down to the water, fills a bucket, runs back to his team, and throws the water in the face of the next teammate. Before the person can throw the water, the waiting teammate must point and yell, "Typhoon!" Each person takes the bucket down to the water and returns to storm his team. The first line to finish is declared the winner.

For safety reasons the throwers should be at least three feet from those to receive the water, and a plastic bucket should be used. On a hot day you will be surprised how many times the kids will want to play this game. *Gary Ogdon*

POP BOTTLE WATER RELAY

For this game you should divide your group into teams of equal size and have the members of each team stand behind the first player. At the signal the last player fills a pop bottle with water from a water source. He then sticks his thumb in the bottle, turns it upside down, and passes it. Each player uses only her thumb to keep the water in, passing the bottle down the line until it reaches the front player. The front player pours the water into an empty container, runs to the back of the line where she refills the pop bottle, and starts it down the line again as she becomes the last player, etc. The first team to fill their empty container wins. *Tony Ward*

PING-PONG BALL FLOAT

For this relay you will need empty coffee cans , Ping-Pong balls, buckets of water, towels, and one person who's willing to get wet for every team participating.

One player lies on his back about 10 yards from his team who are in a single-file line. Place the coffee can (empty) on his stomach or chest. Put the Ping-Pong ball in the coffee can. A bucket full of water goes beside each team.

As the game begins, players use their cupped hands to carry water from their bucket to the coffee can. Each player goes one at a time. As the coffee can fills with water, the Ping-Pong ball rises in the can. As soon as it is high enough, a player tries to remove it from the can with his mouth. The first team to get the Ping-Pong ball out of the can (no hands) and back across the finish line wins. *Larry Jansen*

PLOP PLOP FIZZ FIZZ RELAY

Provide enough Alka-Seltzer tablets for each player. Also, have ready several pitchers of water (enough to fill the cupped hands of team members) and some towels for clean up. Line teams up in relay style and at the signal, send the first one in each line down to the pitchers to grab one, return, and begin pouring water into the cupped hands of each member on their team. The person immediately after the recipient of the water is placing an Alka-Seltzer tablet into the makeshift "cup" of the person before her. The first team to completely dissolve all of their Alka-Seltzer tablets is the winner. *Vein Bauble*

Bucket Brigade

Give each team one empty bucket and one bucket filled with water. Give each player one small paper cup. Place buckets about 30 feet apart. One by one and in order, teammates fill their cups with water, race to the empty bucket, pour their water in it, race back, and tag the next person in line. When the whistle blows, the team with the most water in the once-empty bucket wins.

New Bucket Brigade

To prepare for this activity, you will need to gather enough Styrofoam cups so that each player has one, a plastic milk jug, a large bucket of water, and a small plastic egg (available in craft stores) for each team.

Players stand in single file, forming a bucket brigade with their cups. The large buckets of water are placed at one end of the line. A small plastic egg is put in the milk jug that is placed a short distance from the other end of the line.

A la Bucket Brigade, when the signal is given, the person nearest the bucket dips a cup of water out of the bucket and pours it into the cup of the next person, who passes it to the next person in the same manner. The last person must run to the milk jug, pour in the water, and run to the beginning of the line where he dips a cup of water out of the bucket and passes it. Play continues in this manner until the jug is filled, causing the egg to float to the opening of the jug. The first team to get its egg out (without moving the jug) and toss it into the bucket is the winner.

A one-gallon jug takes about 24 cups to fill. You may want to let team members carry two cups of water to the jug. Have extra eggs on hand in case an egg gets stuck in the jug handle (so the game doesn't have to stop to get the egg free).

For variety the jugs can be made to look like buildings on fire with permanent markers and a plastic figurine can replace the egg. With these changes, the game becomes a fire rescue, giving more meaning to the bucket brigade. *John A. Coen*

Don't Get My Mummy Wet

The object of the game is to make a mummy and carry it over the finish line without getting wet.

Preparing for the game:

Mark off a field about 15 yards by 45 yards. Supply each team with a roll of toilet paper and 10 or more water balloons placed in a bucket. You will also need two sets of numbered index cards, with as many cards in each set as you have teams. For example, if you have four teams, you will have two sets of cards numbered one through four.

Playing the game:

Divide the group into teams of 10 players. Line up the teams at one end of the playing field. Give each team a roll of toilet paper and a bucket of water balloons.

Direct each team to select one person to be the bomber. That player picks a position anywhere on the playing field, takes the bucket to that place,

and sets the bucket down there. Stress that once the bucket is on the ground the bomber cannot move it, and he must stand by the bucket throughout the entire game. If he moves away from the bucket (you may want to set a specific distance), his team will be disqualified. It is the bomber's job to try to get the other teams' mummies wet as they are carried through the field. (It is a good idea not to throw at or near their own mummies.)

Each team selects one person to be the mummy.

At the signal the teams race to wrap their mummies with the whole roll of toilet paper, and to carry the mummies across the field. Everyone on the team except the bomber must always be in contact with the mummy. They can use their bodies to defend their mummies from the water.

Determining the winner:

As the teams come across the finish line, give them an index card from the first set of cards, 1 for the first team across, 2 for the second team across, etc. Then determine which mummy is the driest: 1 for the driest, 2 for the second driest, and so on.

Add the points on both cards to determine the team's total score. The group with the lowest number of points is the winner. *Doug Partin*

NECK COOLER

The objective of Neck Cooler is to successfully pass a waterlogged foam ball down a line of people, using only the neck, chin, and head. This activity is great as a competitive or noncompetitive icebreaker on a hot summer day or as part of an Olympics-type recreation event. It is suitable for small-sized groups.

You will need to gather small softball-size foam balls, one large bucket of ice water, and plenty of towels. Be sure you scope out a convenient water source.

Soak the balls in the bucket of water while you line the group up outside. Place the ball under the chin of the first person in line. The first person passes the ball to the next person in line as quickly as possible. The water temperature motivates the students to pass the ball quickly, and you should encourage speed so the ball has more icy water to give at the end of the line. Only hand each person a towel after they have successfully passed the ball to the next person. The game continues until everyone has been pretty well soaked.

For a competitive twist, have teams with fewer players. The ball will be wetter at the end of the line and so will the players. By having fewer people on the teams, you increase the chances of getting everyone wet.

Another variation of the game includes passing the ball with the chin/neck down the line and then back up to the front. You may want to make it a rule that if the ball drops into the dirt, the person dropping the ball must retrieve it and place the ball, dirt and all, back under her chin and continue. *Michael W. Capps*

FILL MY CUP

For this carnival or lock-in game, you'll need a table, a squirt gun, a small cup (an individual communion cup works fine), and a flat, dense surface that can deflect a stream of water from a squirt gun.

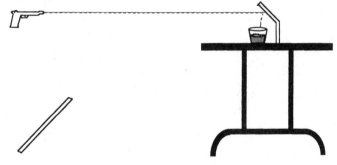

Anchor the small cup to the table with tape, arrange the deflector behind and above the cup (see diagram), and mark a line behind which shooters must stand. Time the shooters; the winner is the one to fill the cup to the line in the least time. Or set up two targets, and have shooters race each other. *Brett Wilson*

ICE-MELTING CONTEST

Each team is given a 25-pound block of ice. Each ice block is weighed in, and the teams are given 10 minutes to try to melt as much of it as possible. No water, fire, crushing, or chipping of the ice is allowed. At the end of 10 minutes, each block is weighed again, and the block that lost the most weight wins. *Bill Flanagan*

WIDE
GAMES

"Wide games" are what we call games requiring teams to strategize, organize, and assign tasks. They call for more than the usual planning, stealth, and skill. Most wide games—sometimes called "adventure games"— have a theme, like spies or secret agents, armies at war, and the like. Most require a good deal of space, such as an open field or a wooded area with places to hide. For suggestions on creating your own wide games, see "On Creating Your Own Wide Games" on page 144.

ALIENS

Loosely based on the movie *Aliens*, this game can be played outside at night in an area with a minimum of light or inside a large darkened building.

Choose three students to be the aliens and two others to be "weapons." If your group is smaller than 15, two aliens and one weapon will work better. All other teens are astronauts.

Before the game begins, the astronauts are confined to a space designated as the brig, while the aliens hide the weapons anywhere in the playing area. Once they're concealed, the weapons are considered inanimate objects; they can't move, speak, or reveal their hiding places in any way. The aliens shouldn't guard the locations of the weapons—it only makes the weapon hiding places obvious.

The game begins when the astronauts are released to search for the weapons. When a weapon is found, the astronaut takes it by the hand to look for the aliens, who can be captured simply by tagging them. When an alien discovers that a weapon has been found, that alien can yell "Weapon! Weapon!" to alert the other aliens, who all hide from the astronauts with weapons.

While the hunt is on for weapons, the aliens are chasing astronauts, who must go directly to the brig if tagged. The astronauts must wait there until they are tagged by another astronaut who hasn't been caught. Don't let the aliens guard the brig, either; the astronauts should be able to be freed easily.

The round is over when all the aliens have been annihilated (the astronauts win), or when the astronauts are all in the brig (the aliens win), or after 20 minutes (the aliens win because this means the weapons were well hidden).

You might want to mark aliens by adorning them with glow-in-the-dark rings (buy them at party shops for a couple bucks apiece). Since the aliens generally have the advantage, this is a great equalizer. *Jason Stuart*

BATTLE FOR THE SAHARA

This is a game for two or more teams in an outdoor setting. Each team has a water container and must transport water across the "Sahara" (playing field) to fill the container. The first to do so wins. Each team

ON CREATING YOUR OWN WIDE GAMES

Create your own game based on your needs, camp location, time of the year, or whatever by using the following guidelines.

• Plan a game with several other people, evaluating every part of it together to see if it will work, be fun, and be safe. Two or three thinking it out together will soon see loopholes in the game, things that need to be clarified, etc. Try to anticipate ways of cheating and cover them with rules. However, be sure not to stamp out all creativity with rules.

• Ask, "Will everyone be able to play in this game till the end? Is it possible the game could be over in a very short time?" Try to make sure the game is challenging enough to last some time but simple enough that people will actually feel they are getting somewhere. For example, make sure some gold can be found easily and some of it is pretty well hidden.

Be very careful to see that people are recycled. For example, when someone loses his life or is imprisoned, there must be a fairly simple way for him to get back into the game again; otherwise, the game will be very boring for him.

• Make sure all boundaries are clear. A person must know when she's safe and when she's not. If the boundaries are clear, disputes will be kept to a minimum. Make use of clear roads and trails, use string to make clear lines. Also, a number of supervisors on hand at all major spots of conflict can help to quickly rule on disputes before they get out of hand. Keep the game moving!

• Try to design games so there is a role for the quieter, nonathletic campers. Anybody can look for treasure in the bush. Adjust your game to your crowd.

• Make your scores high. Instead of one point for a prisoner, make it 1,000 or 10,000. It sounds much more impressive.

• Make sure teams are clearly identifiable; Everyone must be able to tell who's on which team (unless the game specifically involves not knowing). Kids will tend to try to hide their armbands or their tape. Stop that one quickly.

• Watch for safety hazards. Check out areas to be used before each game. Get rid of barbed wire, open wells, dangerous holes, etc. Clearly mark dangerous areas and remind campers of them. Night games in bush are dangerous. Emphasize skulking at night rather than running. Find areas of high grass and low bush where sneaking is more effective than running. In indoor games, no running should be allowed. Players have got to be sneaky, not fast.

• The game is to be played by the rules set down. Most of these games will never work unless players understand the concept of honor. If you are shot, you're dead; if you're clubbed, you must go as a prisoner; if you have been caught, you must give up your gold. Heavily penalize teams that cheat.

• Make sure leaders understand the game clearly. Always have a few counselors helping the campers on each team. Go over the game rules thoroughly with everyone ahead of time. Use a map to clearly illustrate boundaries. Have leaders in control of the areas where

should consist of a general, a bomb, three colonels, four majors, and five or six privates. For a smaller or greater number of players, more majors, colonels, and privates are added with perhaps lieutenants as well. Each player (except the general) has a water cup, gallon container, and each team has a water jug.

Have a specified area where water may be obtained (which may be neutralized so players can avoid capture while filling up). Identify a neutral area around the water jugs, which are located a fair distance away from the water supply, perhaps 1000 to 2000 feet.

Each player (except the general) travels to the water supply area with his cup and gets it full of water. He then travels to the water jug and pours it in. While en route, he may be tagged by a player of one of the opposing teams. A tagging person must also have a cup full of water in order to make her eligible to tag. If a person tagged is of a lower rank, he must empty his cup. If two equal ranks are tagged, they part friends with their cups still full. If the person who is tagged is a higher rank, the tagger must tip hers out. Each person has an identity card with his or her rank marked on it. These can be written out in the team color.

All may tag except the bomb (although the private has no use for tagging, being the lowest rank). The bomb carries water but may tag no one. Anyone tagging the bomb is automatically demoted to private and has his cup emptied. Anyone demoted to private must give up his card to the bomb, who then turns it in to one of the referees at the earliest opportunity.

Any accidental emptying by an opponent gets the offended player a free escort with a full cup to his jug by the offending player. A general may tag without carrying a cup of water (he doesn't have one) and is free to tag others at any time.

It's wise to set a time limit, and the winning team is the one who either has the most water in its jug at the end of the time or who fills it up first. It's wise to have referees along the route to make sure no foul play ensues and that offenses get free escorts properly. *Brett Cane*

points are made or lost.
• It is helpful to get the whole camp excited about the game ahead of time by building team identity—assign team colors, names, signals, etc.

Neil Graham

144

BEAN BAG BALL

This is a wild activity that is great for camps and can be set up like a championship football game. Divide the crowd into two large groups and give them names of schools (make them up). Each "school" is provided plenty of newspapers, tape, magic markers, crepe paper, scissors, poster paint, etc. They have 30 minutes to do the following:

• Prepare a band, complete with uniforms (make them), instruments (anything you can find), drum major, majorettes, etc., plus a march or two that can be hummed (waxed paper on combs help here). One band should be prepared to play the "Star-Spangled Banner."

• Prepare cheerleaders (usually boys dressed like girls), complete with costumes and cheers.

• Prepare a Homecoming Queen with court boys, girls, or mixed). Fix up costumes.

• Prepare a team for Bean-Bag Ball (see following rules). Ordinarily a team of seven plus a coach will do.

• Prepare a half-time program and a crowning of the Homecoming Queen and court.

After each school has done all this, then begin the action as follows:

1. School A Marching Band marches onto the field followed by the team and cheerleaders. An announcer introduces the team. The cheerleaders do their stuff.

2. School B does the same.

3. Leaders ask one band to play the "Star-Spangled Banner."

4. Play the first half of the game (five to seven minutes). Cheerleaders and bands do their stuff too.

5. For the half-time program, School A performs its program and crowns its homecoming queen. Then School B does the same.

6. Play the second half of the game.

7. Have a victory celebration by the winning team.

A good P.A. system and announcer will add a great deal.

Here's how Bean-Bag Ball is played: Two referees are needed with whistles. The playing field can vary in size, but anything larger than a volleyball court will do. There should be a half-way line and at each end of the field a folding chair is placed three feet beyond the goal line. The rules are similar to basketball except the bagholder may take three steps with the bean bag, then he must pass it. Goals are scored by tossing the bean bag between the seat and the seat-back of the chair. *Richard Boyd*

DIAMOND SMUGGLING

This indoor camp game was developed for several reasons:

• Often weather can ruin an outdoor game so that people get wet, muddy, or cold.

• Most camps have plenty of outdoor activities, so less tiring indoor games may be more appropriate.

• Indoor games do not emphasize athletic ability—rather intelligence and sneakiness—thus quieter kids generally like them better. They are very good, also, for adults.

• You can control your campers at night far better with an indoor game than an outdoor one. There is virtually no safety hazard and you know where everyone is.

You will need a fairly large building for this game—a dining hall or large lounge with at least two rooms going off the main room. A school gym will also work.

The dining hall is set up as a cafe in Paris. Paris should reflect the atmosphere of a typical cafe—low lights, some kind of music playing, and food and drinks being served. Some kids may play cards, etc. One of the rooms off the dining hall is the police station and another room (preferably not using the same hallway) is South Africa (the smugglers' den). Use marbles for diamonds.

The players are divided into two teams: the diamond smugglers and the police. The smugglers then break themselves down into two groups—the diamond runners and the diamond smugglers—when they meet privately before the game in the smugglers' den.

Use about 40 diamonds for a game that involves about 40 people on each team.

The object is for the whole smuggling team to circulate from South Africa into Paris and back. The runners, whose names are on paper and are about one-third of the team, are allowed by the leader (an adult) to take a diamond out of South Africa into Paris where they must pass it to a smuggler, who then brings it back to the den and gives it to a diamond buyer (an adult). The team collects 5,000 points per diamond brought back to the den by a smuggler—not a runner. (Runners cannot bring diamonds back from Paris. That's why their names need to be written down so the diamond buyers know the difference between runners and smugglers.) The police never know the difference between runners and smugglers, otherwise they could seize all runners coming in the door at Paris. All the smugglers and runners need to keep circulating back and forth from South Africa to Paris so the police never know who are runners and who are smugglers.

The runners can pass diamonds any way they can devise—in glasses, under the table, in shoes, etc. They can drop a diamond off, and let a smuggler know where it is.

The police are everywhere in Paris (and only in this room). They can arrest anyone they wish on suspicion of possession of stolen diamonds. To arrest someone they simply place a hand on the shoulder of the person they wish to arrest and say, "You're under arrest." The person must go with the officer to the police station—in no way can they resist or try

to ditch a diamond after being arrested. The police officer must accompany his prisoner to the police station. He presents the prisoner at the door, and a detective (adult) takes her inside. The police officer is then free to go. The police station should be a secret place that police can't see into. Here detectives confront the prisoner and she must say whether or not she has a diamond. If she does she must give it up, and the police get 10,000 points for seizure of the diamond, and it's kept there. If the prisoner does not have a diamond, the police lose 4,000 points for falsely arresting the person. In either case the prisoner is free to go out (preferably by another door) into circulation in Paris.

If a police officer can convince a runner that he's a smuggler and get him to give him a diamond, he will simply turn the diamond in at the police station and the police get 10,000 points. If a police officer finds a diamond, he does the same thing.

It is best to run the game 30 to 40 minutes, have a half-time during which the teams change roles (because the police have a tougher job than the smugglers), then run the game for another 30 to 40 minutes. *Neil Graham*

FAMILY GAME

This game is best with a large group (say 80 or so kids) in an indoor setting, such as a gymnasium or recreation hall.

Divide the group into "families" (eight families of 10, for example). Each family should represent a family immigrating to this country from another. In honor of their immigration to their new home, this game can begin with a banquet (sponsored by the Immigration Department), in which all the families are invited. Each family selects a mother and father who name the children all having some resemblance to the mother and father (all blonde, freckles, hats alike, or something). Each family must also prepare a native dance or native song from the country they come from to perform at the banquet. They introduce the family members by their full names to everyone else. The banquet can feature a variety of international dishes to make everyone feel at home.

At the conclusion of the banquet, the Minister of Immigration gives a little speech and presents each family with $2,000 in cash (play money made up of packets of $50, $100, $500, and $1,000 denomin-ations) and gives jobs to about six members of each family (a card with a particular occupation written down on it with the salary stated at the bottom; for example, a card might say: "This certifies that you are a qualified plumber. Salary: $8,000 per year.").

Each family is told by the Minister of Immigration that the government will keep close watch on them and that only those families that succeed in their jobs will be allowed to remain in the country. After the banquet is cleared away, the game begins.

In the course of the game, 15 minutes represents a year. At the end of each year, there is a five-minute break when the families meet together in a specified place for discussion.

At the beginning of each year (indicated by a whistle or bell) each member of the family with a job goes to an area of the room marked with the appropriate job description. For instance, there should be a medical center (for doctors), a trade center, a funeral home, etc.

Also, at the beginning of each year, the father goes to the government desk and picks up his family's list of problems (see sample "problem card" below) which must be solved during that year. At this time he also gives the government a list of which members of his family have what jobs.

In the first year, the problems are few, but as the years go by, the problems get heavier and heavier. The list might contain from five to 12 problems per family that the father has to solve. For example, his house might have plumbing problems—he might need to build a new bathroom. He might have a leaky roof, need new furniture, or need the services of a doctor. There can be deaths in the family—grandmothers, uncles, aunts, children—and a funeral director would have to be consulted, along with a minister, perhaps a doctor, hospital, lawyer about the will, etc.

Problem Cards may look like this:

Year One
- Obtain a place to live
- Get a job
- Obtain a form of transportation for personal use

Year Two
- Pay rent if you do not own a house
- Succeed at job
- Wheels need balancing—see a mechanic
- Buy color TV—see furniture store
- Blown fuse—see an electrician
- Girlfriend gets sick—see florist

For every problem that is listed, there must be an appropriate job to solve the problem. The father may either assign someone else or go himself to the various job areas and have the problem solved by a person who is qualified to do so.

To get a problem solved, a qualified plumber, for instance, signs that all the plumbing work has been done. He may charge you according to how difficult the problem seems to be to him. The father then pays for the plumber to sign and the signature is put on the problem.

At the end of each year, the government examines the problem list of each father to see that everything has been taken care of and that only people who have the right type of job have signed for the work done. If everything is in order, the father is given the next year's list; if he does not have everything done, he may be fined several thousand dollars, maybe even up to $10 or $20 thousand dollars because of the seriousness of not getting certain things done. Then he may be given next year's list, and he must go and solve the new problems.

There can also be a Government Employment Center where new jobs are for sale. Occasionally it can be announced that there is severe unemployment and every family has to turn in several jobs. This keeps the job market floating around, making it possible for families to improve their position—or to get wiped out, as the case may be. The Employment Center also sells B.A.s, M.A.s and Ph.D.s for fairly high sums. Plumbers who have a B.A. get 25 percent more salary each year. The B.A. is stamped by the Government on the job card. An M.A. means 50 percent more salary, and a Ph.D. means 100 percent more.

If you have, say, 80 people, you would need almost 60 jobs, thus leaving some members of each family free to solve problems. During the annual break the family may plan for the next year, look at the next year's list of problems, and work out who is going to solve them. This is also time for counting money and for going to the bank where all salaries are paid. The bank has to have a great supply of play money. Occasionally, hit the families with taxes as well. They have to pay the government a set amount, or a percentage of their income.

You can run the game for five 15 minute years and the family that comes out economically the best is the winner.

It is important to be fair when handing out the jobs at the beginning of the game. Make sure that the high-paying jobs such as doctors, lawyers, and dentists are spread evenly among the families so that no family has a tremendous advantage to begin with. Normally there should be three or four doctor jobs, three or four dentists, etc., so that there will be a good deal of competition in bidding between members of a profession to solve problems. This keeps the prices down and provides a lot of entertainment; however, you may have several professions where there are only one or two jobs available, such as garbage collectors, funeral directors, and ministers. This creates a monopoly for

certain families, with prices sky-rocketing. This makes the game much more entertaining.

This game can fit well into a later discussion on the family and enable you to talk about exclusive and inclusive families and the whole problem of competition in our society. "Do unto others as you would have them do unto you" becomes a very real principle when kids realize that what they charge for a plumbing job (comparatively), may also be charged them when they are burying a loved one.

Neil Graham

HIDE THE COUNSELOR

This is another good camp game. It is merely a game of hide-and-seek for big boys and girls. Make the counselors worth points for team competition. Give one counselor an extra high point value for variety's sake. This could possibly be the camp director. All the counselors then hide. Kids must find the counselors within a given time limit.

Here are some rules:
• Counselors get 15 minutes to hide.
• Kids get 15 minutes to search.
• Kids must tag counselors to catch them.
• No hiding inside buildings.
• When time is up, remaining counselors come out free.

One variation on this game is to give kids water balloons, which must be used to tag counselors.

FUGITIVE

This game is played at night and is a variation of hide-and-seek. The group is divided into two teams: the Fugitives and the FBI. The FBI agents are equipped with flashlights. The Fugitives are given several minutes to hide. After the time limit is up, the FBI agents try to find the Fugitives.

The Fugitives have a certain amount of time (anywhere from 10 to 30 minutes) in which they must reach home base (which can be any designated area).

If a Fugitive has a light shined on him and has his name called out as he attempts to hide or reach home base, then he goes to jail. If he makes it to home base, the Fugitive team gets 10 points. If he is caught by the FBI, then the FBI gets the 10 points.

It may be wise to set a distance of 25 to 40 feet around home base which is off limits to FBI agents.

To make the game more difficult, arm the FBI agents with water balloons or squirt guns with which they must hit Fugitives before making an arrest. If the kids don't know each other's names, then the FBI agents can simply call out some other identifying trait, clothing, or whatever.

After one game, play again with the teams reversing roles. *Fred Winslow*

HIRED GUN

Each person needs a squirt gun or a rubber-tipped toy dart gun. To begin the game, each person writes his or her name on a piece of paper cut into a tombstone shape, with RIP at the top. All tombstones are put into a hat, and everyone draws the name of the person she has been hired to kill.

The players are then released to go out alone and plan their strategy, hide, or whatever. When the whistle is blown, the hunting begins. Each player tries to find the person she has been hired to gun down and to shoot her with the squirt or dart gun. For a shot to be legal, no one else may be present at the time. (It must be done secretly, so that only the victim knows that she has been knocked off.)

Players must carry their tombstones with them at all times. When players successfully kill their victims, they must autograph their tombstones. The victims are eliminated from the game. Then the tombstone is posted so everyone can see who is still in the game.

When players are eliminated, they give their tombstones (the name of the person they were trying to kill) to the players who shot them. Those names become new targets for the hot shots.

If you want the game to have a less violent theme, call it "Kisser." When a person is shot with the squirt gun (or hit with a water balloon), she has been kissed rather than killed. *Dan Gray*

HOLY MAN

The gurus in your group will love this hide-and-seek game, perfect for summer evenings. Select one of your teens to be the "Holy Man," who—dressed in an identifying robe or hat—takes a lit candle and hides somewhere within the boundaries of the game (although he can move around at will and hide somewhere new). When the Holy Man is settled, the other kids—each armed with a squirt gun and an unlit candle—spread out to find him.

When kids discover the Holy Man, they light their own candles from his and then, by stealth more than speed, try to get back to a designated home base before their candles are extinguished by others' squirt guns. (The Holy Man's candle cannot be extinguished by other players.) If their flames get doused, they must return to the Holy Man to relight their candles. The first player to arrive at home base with a lit candle is the winner. *Ann Smith*

HOUNDS AND HARES

This is best played at night. Two teams are chosen. The Hares are given 100 sheets of newspaper. They leave base five minutes before the Hounds gives chase. The Hares affix a sheet of newspaper at eye level approximately every 100 feet. The Hares must use all their newspaper and then get back to base before the Hounds can overtake them. If they safely make it back to base, they win. *Jerry Summers*

RIVER RAID

This game is best played in a big church with lots of corridors, staircases, and the like. Divide into two teams. Both teams are armed with rubber bands and a few paper bullets, as illustrated.

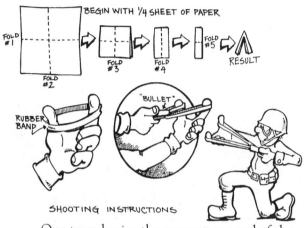

SHOOTING INSTRUCTIONS

One team begins the game at one end of the church, and the other team begins at the other end. The object of the game is for the two teams to change positions—but they must follow the same trail to get there. This is a lot like Chinese checkers. On the way they can eliminate opposing team members by shooting them with their rubber band slingshots.

You can add to the excitement of the game by having more than one route, playing in the dark, and so on. There will be lots of skulking, some huge shoot-outs, and strategies for offense and defense.

Make sure kids don't shoot each other in the face. Although these rubber band paper-shooters are reasonably safe, there is a slight chance of getting shot in the eye. If you prefer not to take that risk, you can substitute simple tagging for shooting. *Jim Walton*

SKIZBOMANIA

Here's a search-and-destroy game in the dark—squirt guns are the weapons, and the targets are pages or pieces of pages from paint-with-water coloring books attached to players' backs. After the battle, the defeated platoon is the one with most hits—and the hits will be obvious when the lights are turned on again.

You can make the game as elaborate or as simple as you want with these modifications:

• Play it in a pitch-dark room in any case. If some indication of players' whereabouts are wanted, each kid can wear a strip of glow-in-the-dark tape on a headband or pinned to his front or back. Or use a strobe light.
• If you want teams identifiable in the dark, arrange a few small glow-strips in a team pattern.
• For more accurate scoring, cut the coloring-book pages into quarter-sized circles; then glue, tape, or staple them onto a paper towel, which is pinned to the back or front of a player. Then again, players can simply wear whole or half pages of coloring books pinned to them, and scoring can be more general.

Although it's not necessary, it is convenient to have a refill place for the squirt guns in the same room. Each game could be longer, too. *Steve Sayer*

MURDER MYSTERY

• **Directions.** In this game the kids are detectives questioning suspects in an effort to find the killer of Mr. John Stone. The five suspects (Mr. Mun, janitor; Steve Stone, John's brother; Sam Swade, lawyer; Mrs. Stone, John's wife; and Ms. Wright, secretary) are prepared ahead of time to act their parts using the scripts provided (pages 153-154). They should come in costumes—the secretary looking seductive, the lawyer shady, the janitor in overalls, and so on. The remaining players are divided into groups of five or six detectives and will attempt to solve the mystery by working within their groups.

The game begins with everyone seeing the scene of the murder (see "Setting Up the Murder Scene" on page 151) and hearing the scripted opening comments given by the host (on page 152). After the opening, each suspect leaves for a separate room, and the groups of detectives move from room to room questioning them (one group in a room at a time, with a time limit of five or 10 minutes per visit). Groups may visit any suspect as many times as they like.

At the conclusion of the game, all groups return to the scene of the murder and write on a piece of paper who they think killed John Stone and how and why they think the murder took place. The game leader then reads all the solutions offered by the kids as well as the solution provided (see "Solution to Murder Mystery" on page 155).

The success of this game lies with the actors playing the five suspects. Skillful youths may play these parts, but it may work out better with adults. Before the game is played, the suspects meet to listen to each others' scripts and hear the solution to the mystery. During the game itself the detectives will ask many questions not covered by the scripts, and although the suspects may say, "The question you asked is not relevant," suspects may also ad-lib as long as it does not conflict with or give away the solution. This can only be done if they already know each others' material.

Each suspect's script is divided into an alibi and one or more confessions. Suspects tell their alibis to every group, but they only offer their confession if the detectives can prove (by quoting evidence from other suspects) that the suspect being questioned is lying. For example, many suspects will claim that they were not at the office that night, but the janitor will place them all at the scene. When the detectives tell the suspects that the janitor testifies to seeing them at the office, the suspects spill their guts, giving the second part of their script.

The suspects must use discretion in their answers. If they are stingy with information, the game will go on too long; if they too readily tell all, the detectives will catch on too quickly. The janitor's first part is rather simple, but the key is when he says that he found the body while checking to see if John and his friends had left. The janitor gives his second part only when the detectives ask if he saw others there.

• **Setting Up the Murder Scene.** The scene is a business office containing a desk and a table (or bookshelf) holding an aquarium. The office is topsy-turvy from an apparent struggle. Papers and file folders are strewn about the room and on the desk. Clearly visible among the papers on the floor is a broken picture frame containing a photo of the actress who plays the part of Mrs. Stone. On the desk is an agenda showing meeting times as follows: secretary 8:00 p.m., Steve Stone 8:30 p.m., Sam Swade 9:15 p.m. The aquarium is tipped over with the gravel falling off the edge of the table. Add some broken glass around it, and on the floor beneath it place some dead fish (from a local pet store's casualties) or cutouts of fish. Also below the aquarium trace the outline of a person with either chalk or masking tape to indicate where the body was found. Add some ketchup, broken glass, and water around the outline of the head. *John McLendon*

WELLS FARGO

To play this game successfully you will need plenty of room to run and good terrain in which to hide (lots of trees, bushes, hills, etc.). You will also need at least 50 players (or even as many as 1,000). Enforce rules strictly in order to ensure safety. Despite the risks, this is one of the most exciting camp games ever created.

Create two teams: the lawmen and the robbers. Kids can dress as if they are living in the wild west in the 1800s (provide costumes, western hats, cardboard sheriff badges, bandanas, etc., if you want). In the center of an open field, mark off an eight-by-eight foot area that becomes the bank. A large garbage can could be used as the bank, if you prefer. You will also need to prepare a number of bags of gold—sacks filled with rocks. They should be light enough that they can be carried by one person or tossed from one person to another. You will also need a piece of masking tape for each person.

Players are to wear the tape in a prominent spot (perhaps their arms). Mark the lawmen's tape with a large, colorful O and the robbers' tape with an X to distinguish teams and to represent paper money.

To begin, lawmen have 10 minutes to hide with the sacks of gold. When the robbers are released, the lawmen are to try to make their way to the bank to make a deposit. Meanwhile they are being hunted down by the robbers who are to steal the gold and the tape from each lawman's arm. Lawmen are to try to take tape from the robbers when possible. Players can take gold and tape from opponents by overpowering them. Once the tape is taken, the player is dead and out of the game.

OPENING COMMENTS TO DETECTIVES

This is the office of John Stone, who was murdered last night. The janitor found him on the floor at 10:00 p.m. The cause of death was a blow to the back of his head, and the time of death was between 8:00 and 10:00 p.m. From the agenda on the desk, we know that he was working late and was to see his secretary at 8:00 p.m., his brother Steve Stone (who was his business partner) at 8:30 p.m., and his lawyer Sam Swade at 9:15 p.m. We have all three of these people here for you to question. We also have Mr. Stone's wife here as well as the janitor who found his body.

Your job is to find out who killed John Stone and how and why they did it. That is, by evidence at the scene and from what you learn from the suspects, you must prove who the murderer is, the motive for the murder, and the method of the murder. Once you know this information, write it on a paper. We will read all your conclusions at _____, then I will tell you who is right.

time

You are investigators. When you get some evidence, use it to get more information. One or more of these people will be lying, but if you confront them with evidence, they will come clean. For instance, if you find out that one of the suspects made a death threat, do not say to that person, "Did you say you would kill John Stone?" Say instead, "I have a witness who will testify that you said you were going to kill John Stone."

The suspects will not have answers to all your questions. If they seem to be making up answers to some of your questions, it is not always a clue that they are lying. They may be trying to give an appropriate answer that will not at the same time lead you off track. They may also decline to answer saying that your question is not relevant to the case.

MRS. STONE, JOHN'S WIFE

Alibi: All I know is my husband was a good man, and I don't know why anyone would want to kill him. I was home all night long until 10 o'clock when the police called and (*she begins to cry*) told me John had been killed.

Confession: I had a phone call from someone. He would not give his name, but he said my husband was having an affair with his secretary. I had suspected it for a long time and had told several of my friends that if I found out it was true I would kill him. When I got the call I went to his office. I was very angry, but I was not going to kill him. When I got there, the place was a mess. Papers were everywhere, my picture was smashed, and the carpet was soaked from the broken aquarium. It looked like there had been a terrible fight. John was (*attempting to retain emotional control of herself*) lying there—blood all over the back of his head. I can still see him in my mind—his blank expression and all those fish wiggling around him. I couldn't have killed him. I loved him.

MR. STEVE STONE, BROTHER TO JOHN

Alibi: I had a meeting set up with my brother to finalize some papers on an account we had been working on. I was to meet him at his office at 8:30, but I had an emergency come up and was not going to be able to make the meeting. I called several times to tell John I wasn't coming and that he should make whatever decisions had to be made and that I'd back whatever he thought was best, but I never got an answer at his office. I never left my office. In fact, I was still there when the police called to tell me John had been murdered.

Confession: Yes, I was at John's office at 8:30 for our meeting. When I walked in he was on the floor. There were signs of a struggle—some pictures were broken, some papers were scattered on the floor. I went to look at John, and there was a small pool of blood from a blow to the back of his head. I would have called the police, but my brother and I had been having some problems.

You see, John was greedy for power and money (*getting angry now*). He was trying to cut me out of the business. I had been working with our lawyer, Sam Swade, to steal the control of the company from John.

There were some papers in John's office we had falsified, and I thought it would be best if I got them out of the office before I called the police. But I couldn't find them. That's when I knew Sam Swade must have killed John. He was a crook to begin with, and there's no telling what kind of deals he's been pulling. I didn't know what to do, so I left and went back to my office as if I'd never left there, and waited until the police called.

I didn't kill him. He was already dead when I got there. I couldn't kill him. He was my brother! But I'd bet my life Sam Swade is behind this.

MS. SANDY WRIGHT, SECRETARY

Alibi: I came by the office at 8 o'clock to drop off some papers for Mr. Stone. He needed them for some meetings he was having that evening. I was only there for a minute. He was on the phone, so I left them on his desk. He said thanks, and I left. That's all I knew until the police called me at my home around 10 o'clock to tell me Mr. Stone was dead.

Confession: Yes, I was having an affair with Mr. Stone. When I came in to drop off the papers, he told me it was all over—I was being let go Monday and he told me not to ever set foot in the place again. He treated me like some undesirable business deal. I was hurt and angry. I pulled his wife's pictures off the wall and broke them. Then I started yelling at him. He started toward me from around the desk. I didn't even want him to touch me, so I pushed him away, and he tripped over the lamp cord and hit his head.

Then he just laid there and didn't move at all. I didn't mean to kill him. It was an accident (*starts crying*). You can ask the janitor. He heard the pictures breaking and heard the yelling and came into the office just as John fell and hit his head. He told me he knew it was an accident. He said for me to go home and he would make it look like a break in and robbery. I did it because I looked so guilty and was afraid. I swear I did not mean to kill him.

MR. SAM SWADE, LAWYER

Alibi: I was scheduled to meet with John Stone at 9:15 to finalize the signing of some business papers that he and his brother were working on. But my paging service left a message with me that someone had called and cancelled the appointment. She didn't say who called—I just assumed it was John. The message said the meeting would be rescheduled for the next day sometime, so I never went to John's office. The first thing I heard was when the police called me at home around 10 o'clock.

Confession: Yes, I did go to John's office at 9:15. When I walked in, John was lying on the floor. Things were messed up—papers all over the floor,

some pictures were broken. I went around to look at John closer. There was a little blood on the floor, which seemed to come from the back of his head. I could tell by looking at him he was dead.

I was going to call the police, but first I had to check on some records. Steve Stone had been having some power struggles with his brother, and I had helped him falsify some records so he could gain more power in the company. When I looked, though, the records were gone. Steve was the only one who knew about them, so I knew he had to be the one who took them. I knew he was hungry for power. In fact, although I can't prove it, I think he

was also blackmailing John.

Two days before his death John told me somebody was blackmailing him. He had been having an affair with his secretary, Sandy Wright, and told me someone was getting him for big bucks to keep it from his wife. He asked me for advice on how to get out without legal problems. I told him the first step was to break the relationship with Ms. Wright and get her as far away from him as possible. In fact, he was going to do that when she brought the papers by the night of his murder.

I'm innocent. I didn't kill John Stone. He was dead when I got there. The more I think about it, the more the finger points straight at Steve Stone.

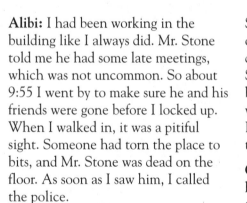

MR. MUN, JANITOR

Alibi: I had been working in the building like I always did. Mr. Stone told me he had some late meetings, which was not uncommon. So about 9:55 I went by to make sure he and his friends were gone before I locked up. When I walked in, it was a pitiful sight. Someone had torn the place to bits, and Mr. Stone was dead on the floor. As soon as I saw him, I called the police.

Confession A: *[Use the following speech only if the detectives ask who you saw come in.]* Well, his secretary came by to drop off some papers. I was cleaning the hall. She went in and came right back out. Then a while later I saw Mr. Stone's brother going through the main lobby. I'm not sure how long he was there because I didn't see him leave. A little later I saw Mr.

Stone's lawyer, Sam Swade, getting out of his car in the parking lot, but I didn't see him leave, either. Mrs. Stone's wife must have also been there because her coat was on the rack when I went to lock up around 9:50. But it wasn't there when I had cleaned the hall at 8 o'clock.

Confession B: Okay, I was cleaning the hall when Ms. Wright came by with the papers. She went into the office. After a little while I heard glass break and some yelling. I came down the hall and walked into the office. As I did I saw Mr. Stone coming around the desk toward Ms. Wright. As he got to her she pushed him away and he tripped and fell backward. His head hit the aquarium, and it busted everywhere. Then he fell to the floor. I checked him for his pulse, but he was dead.

I knew it was an accident, so I told Sandy—ah, Ms. Wright—to go home, that it was an accident, and that I would make it look like someone had robbed the place. She left, but before I could do anything, Mr. Stone's brother showed up. He saw his brother, then snooped around the place looking for something. He finally left. When I was sure he had gone, I started again to make the place look like a robbery. But then Mr. Swade came down the hall. He looked all over the room also, but didn't leave with anything. Not long after that Mr. Stone's wife came and then ran out. After that I just messed the place up a little and called the police. I was only trying to help Ms. Wright.

SOLUTION TO MURDER MYSTERY

John Stone was in his office at 8 o'clock when his secretary Ms. Wright (with whom he had been having an affair) came in. On the counsel of his lawyer, John broke off the relationship with her and let her go as his secretary to avoid being blackmailed. She reacted violently, smashing the picture of John's wife. John came around the desk to try and restrain her, but she pushed him away. He tripped, fell backward, and hit his head on the aquarium stand. He fell unconscious on the floor, but was not dead. The janitor came in just as John hit his head and fell to the floor. He saw it was an accident and told Ms. Wright to go home and he would make it look like a robbery.

Before he was able to do this, however, Steve Stone came in. Seeing the mess and his brother on the floor, he went to the file and took out some papers he had falsified so that he could steal the company from his brother. He felt that if they were found, it would make him look guilty of killing John. He was sure that the lawyer had killed his brother and was going to pin it on him.

He then went back to his office and waited there as if he had never left.

Again the janitor was unable to finish making the place look like a robbery because the lawyer came in. He also looked for the papers that Steve had taken. When he could not find them, he figured that Steve was the murderer and that he was going to use the papers to frame him. So he also left and created an alibi.

Soon after this John's wife received a call telling her that he was having an affair. When she came down she was out for blood, but it had already been shed. When she saw the mess she was afraid that it would look like she had indeed killed her husband in a fit of rage. She also left, but what she saw was the main piece of evidence. She said that the fish were alive ("wiggling around him") at 9:50, which meant that the aquarium could not have been broken by the secretary at 7 o'clock. However, no one else had mentioned the aquarium being broken—except the janitor. Mr. Mun said Ms. Wright pushed John, and his head hit the aquarium, breaking it.

When Sam Swade left John's office, the janitor again tried to mess up the room. His intent was not simply to make it look like a robbery, but to really rob John Stone. Since he believed his blackmail scheme was already destroyed (Mr. Mun thought John was dead), he decided to remove the safe keys from John's body, clean the place out, and pin the murder and robbery on Ms. Wright, Steve Stone, or Sam Swade. But as he searched John's pockets for the keys, John began to wake up. Mr. Mun picked John up enough to strike his head again, this time truly killing John Stone.

To cover his tracks, he called John's wife and told her John was having an affair. He knew she suspected it and had overheard her threatening John in the office. He did not anticipate that it would be her testimony that would put him away.

The bags of gold are worth 1000 points each. Each piece of tape, which represents paper money, is worth 100 points each. Lawmen must get the gold into the bank. It is worthless to them if they still have it in their possession at the end of the game.

Robbers don't have to put it in the bank to collect their points. All they have to do is capture it and stash it someplace until the game is over. However, that stash can be raided by the lawmen.

The game can last 30 to 45 minutes or so. At the end of the game the teams add up their scores, based on how many pieces of tape they have and how many bags of gold they put in the bank or captured. The team with the most points wins.

As a safety measure, guys cannot steal tape from girls. It is best for kids to travel in groups and work out their strategies.

• **How the West Was Fun.** For this variation of Wells Fargo, divide into four (or more) teams. Give each team different colored armbands. Each player also gets a masking tape "scalp," which can be placed on each person's forehead or somewhere else (like the armband). Each tape scalp should be marked with an initial or some other mark that identifies the team. Invent western-style names like the Miners and the Outlaws.

Like Wells Fargo the object of the game is to find bags of gold and return them to the bank and to kill people by capturing scalps. The bags of gold (rocks painted with gold paint) are hidden prior to the game all over the playing area in difficult-to-find places. Just before the game starts, everybody takes off and spreads out. Then the whistle or horn blows, indicating that the game is on. Players get 1,000 points for every scalp they collect but establish limitations such as—

• Cowboys can only kill Outlaws
• Indians can only kill Cowboys
• Miners can only kill Indians
• Outlaws can only kill Miners

Anyone killing a player from the wrong team is automatically dead himself. Once a player's scalp is gone, she is temporarily out of the game and must go to Boot Hill for five minutes. Then she gets a new scalp and may re-enter the game.

If a bag of gold is found, it must get to the bank to get points for it. A bag of gold is worth 5,000 points. Players may steal the gold while it is on its way to the bank. Any method of stealing the gold is legal (except guys can't steal the gold from gals). No player may come within 50 yards of the bank unless he is carrying the gold or is chasing someone who is.

The game is over when the time limit is up, or when all the bags of gold have been found and turned in for points. The team with the most points is the winner.

Another twist is to hide one bag of fool's gold (non-painted rocks or rocks that have some secret marking on them). Any team that brings it in loses 5,000 points. *Doug Newhouse*

BUZZARDS AND EAGLES

Divide players into four teams and give them names like "Buzzards," "Eagles," "Turkeys," and other bird names. Then designate a headquarters for each team that is an equal distance from what will be called the "Central Nest." The object of the game is for each team to transport eggs from their headquarters to the Central Nest. Each egg is worth 1,000 points.

Give the teams an equal number of eggs—real ones or plastic, colored eggs. Each team will also need a portable nest—that is, a common bathroom plunger! Finally, every player needs a feather or a strip of cloth that is tucked into the waist as in flag football. Don't allow kids to tie them to their jeans or tuck them in so far that they're hidden.

Once a team has its eggs at its own headquarters, it may—on your signal—begin transporting them to the Central Nest, but only in the portable nest. Obviously, several trips back and forth will be required for each team, since the portable nest will only hold a few eggs.

Players may try to keep other teams from transporting their eggs by plucking them—that is, by pulling their flags, flag-football style. Anyone who is plucked must report to the bird hospital and see the vet for five minutes before returning to play.

If players pluck someone who is carrying a portable nest with eggs, they can take those eggs to their own headquarters and use them to score points for their team. However, players cannot steal another team's portable nest or break it. Players are also forbidden to enter another team's headquarters. To keep this game from getting too rough, you should rule out tackling or holding players down in order to pluck them.

Besides the score for eggs, you can award a team additional points each time they pluck someone. Just have the plucker and the pluckee report in.

If you're at camp with a large staff of counselors, designate them as buzzards, whose only job is to run around plucking eagles and to make them drop their eggs as they run for the Central Nest. (In this case, there would be only two teams.)

Teen Valley Ranch

CHAOS VERSUS CONTROL

This is an outdoor spy game that is best played where there is plenty of room and good hiding places. It should be played at night and preferably in an area with a lot of trees and high grass. You can use several large flashlights (controlled by counselors) to sweep the entire area to give a searchlight effect to the game. Divide into two teams: the Chaos agents and the Control agents. (You can name the teams anything. The names are not important to the game.) The two teams should wear different colored armbands to distinguish them. The Chaos agents try to leave the U.S. by reaching a landing strip where their planes are to pick them up. The Control agents try to capture or eliminate the Chaos agents by hitting them with a stocking full of flour. The set up should look like this:

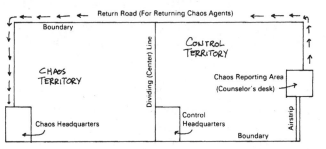

The Chaos agents are safe when in their own territory. They simply have to sneak through Control territory to get to the airstrip located behind Control territory. If they manage to get through, they report to a counselor sitting at a desk on the airstrip. They are safe once they get to the airstrip. When they arrive there, they turn over to the counselor a set of secret plans (an envelope marked "SST" or "APOLLO," etc.). The Chaos team gets 1000 points for each envelope delivered to the airstrip counselor. Chaos agents may then return to their own headquarters via a path around Control territory to get a new set of plans and try to sneak through again. Control agents may patrol that path to make sure Chaos people are only going back and not coming to the airstrip.

Control agents can only be in their own territory and they must try to spot and club a Chaos agent with their nylon (or newspaper, water balloon, paper bag full of mud, or whatever.) If they hit a Chaos agent, the Control agent takes his prisoner to Control headquarters and the Chaos agent must give up his plans. The Control team gets 2000 points for each set of plans seized. The Chaos agent is then set free to try again. Adult Counselors should keep score, hand out the plans, etc. *Neil Graham*

THE GOLD RUSH

This is a rather elaborate camp game. It may be played during a whole afternoon and evening. The entire camp is turned into a kind of "boom town," with the sheriff's office, assayer's office, Henrietta's Hash House, mayor's home, jail, claims office, etc.

The camp should be divided up into nine teams. Each team is given a map of the forest around the camp (divided into nine claims) and are given an opportunity to decide which one they want to mine on. Did they want the largest claim or the smallest? The closest to the jail or not? The one closest to the other claims or one off by itself?

On each claim hide about 75 to 100 pieces of gold (rocks of varying sizes painted gold). Each piece of gold has the claim number on it (for example, the gold on Claim No. 3 has a "3" on it). The gold may be hidden under logs, put on tree limbs, be scattered in the thickest bush. The claims should be dense forest at least 100x50 yards wide. They should also be clearly marked by trails.

All the teams meet together in a clearing and select a runner to run for them to the claims office to stake the claim they want. Begin the race with a cap gunshot, and the runners race to stake their claim first come, first served. The last one gets what is left over. After being given the claim slip at the claims office, they run back to their teams and tell them what claim they have. Then the teams head for the claims and start hunting for gold. Each team is given a number of potato sacks to store their gold in. They have to keep all their gold on their claim until the end of the game.

After 20 minutes of mining their claims, a bell is rung and the teams are now allowed to jump other claims—either to search for gold not yet found or to raid the main stockpile of another team. Incentive to claim jump may be given by saying that you will award a team double the points for gold with another team's claim number on it.

Each team may defend its claim by using water guns filled with water colored with red food coloring. Give each team six water guns and two pails of red water. All claim jumpers must wear a colored team armband to identify themselves. They can only shoot on another's claim, not on any trail or road dividing the claims. If one team manages to get some red on a

claim jumper, they blow a whistle and the sheriff or a deputy (the camp work crew or leadership) comes to the scene. All wounded claim jumpers must cooperate once they are shot and are taken by the sheriff's posse to the jail—two large concentric circles of flour, 10 and 20 yards in diameter. The space between the outer and inner circle is no man's land, while the inner circle is the jail itself where the prisoners are kept. Several deputies patrol the prison circumference with water guns and watch for people trying to break prisoners out.

When a prisoner is brought in, put a big black O on one hand in indelible ink to indicate that he is a prisoner; his team number is recorded along with his name. His team must break him out within 20 minutes of his arrest—by sending a teammate to run into the prison to touch him, whereupon both are free to leave. A person trying to break someone out of jail may not be shot by a deputy till she enters the clearly marked no man's land. She is safe if she reaches the inner circle

without being shot. If she is shot, she, too, is made a prisoner and her team number recorded. However, if a player is freed from prison by a comrade, he still has an "O" on his hand and can be shot by bounty hunters because he is now a fugitive from justice. He may be shot on any trail or road or any claim except his own and the team shooting him is given $1,000 at the end of the game for bringing him back to the jail.

If a team fails to break one of their players out of jail before the 20 minutes is up, the prisoner is released and a big red "X" is painted through the "O" on the back of his hand to show that he has been properly released. However, his team is charged $2,000 bail for his release. He can't be shot by bounty hunters because of the "X" on his hand. However, if he is shot claim jumping again, an "O" will be put on the other hand. It generally pays to break your teammates out of jail.

Allow the claim jumping to go on for about an hour. Then ring the bell and the game is over. At the end of the game, each team brings all its gold into the assayer's office where it is carefully stored until after supper.

Then hold a boom town supper complete with an evening of skits, chorus lines, etc. The evening ends by having the assayer, with the sheriff guarding him, weigh up all the gold (doubling the weight of stolen gold). He then writes out a check for the amount of gold, and the team leader cashes this at the nearby bank. The banker can pay off any way she wants in chocolate bars or other kinds of food. (How about stacks of chocolate coins covered in gold wrapping?) She may also "double-cross" the teams somewhat by having some of the gold thrown out by the assayer as fool's gold. How can he distinguish? All the gold has numbers on it. Those pieces with numbers in green are true gold; those with numbers in blue are fool's gold. *Neil Graham*

THE HUDSON'S BAY VERSUS NORTHWEST FUR TRADING COMPANY

Start with an outline of the history of the battle for fur trading territory between these two companies. The two teams are given adjacent territory and different colors of armbands to distinguish them.

Clearly mark the dividing line between territories. The object of the game is for each team to find furs on its own territory and deliver them to its headquarters in the other's territory. Thus the voyagers must carry a load of furs (up to 10 each) across the line through enemy territory to the safety of their post (a natural clearing, large circle, camp shelter, etc.). Once they cross into enemy territory, they can be killed by the other team and their furs seized.

The furs can be strips of cardboard 2"x6" pieces of wood of the same length. Spread about 200 pieces throughout each territory. All the Hudson's Bay fur should be marked with an "H" and spread in their territory; all the Northwest fur should be with an "N" and spread in their territory.

Instruct the teams that they may search for furs on their own territory and then deliver them to their headquarters—or they can send team members into enemy territory to hunt for fur and deliver it to their headquarters. Of course, as soon as a person crosses the line, he can be killed (his armband is taken by the enemy). No fur can be taken into a headquarters by a person missing an armband. Players who are killed must surrender any fur they have to the enemy and return to their own lines to pick up a new armband and start again.

The game is very effective in bush country particularly in winter or at night because the fur is easily hidden and it involves a lot of skulking. The center boundary line must be clearly marked, especially at night; a couple of bonfires are sufficient.

The game is stopped at an arbitrary time limit (45 minutes or so) and the furs counted to see who won.

To encourage risking their lives, a team may be awarded double points for every enemy fur they deliver to their headquarters. *Neil Graham*

INFILTRATION

Infiltration needs to be played after dark, in an area where there are no artificial lights. (Even moonlight makes this game difficult.) It is also best played in a wooded area.

Initial Set-up: A perimeter is designated along easily recognizable objects (trees, fallen logs,

rocks, etc.). The radius should be between 70 and 100 yards, depending upon the size of the group. In the center of the perimeter is a flag. The group is divided into two teams, the Defenders and the Infiltrators.

Object: It is the goal of the Infiltrators to sneak into the area inside the perimeter, obtain the flag, and sneak out, without being killed. It is the object of the Defenders to prevent any Infiltrator from taking the flag.

Equipment: All Defenders will need flashlights. (The type with a button that allows short bursts of light are best.) And something designated as a flag is needed.

Rules for the Defenders:
• No Defender can enter inside the perimeter.
• The Defenders kill an Infiltrator by shooting him with his flashlight. The flashlights cannot be on for more than one second per shot. (Flashlights can't be used as searchlights.)
• Any Defender using his flashlight as a searchlight or repeatedly firing his flashlight will be deemed out of ammo for five minutes.
• Once a Defender believes that he has a kill, he may keep his flashlight positioned on the spot where he believes his victim is. A judge will check to see if there is anyone there. (The beam must be on the victim.)

Rules for the Infiltrators:
• Once an Infiltrator knows that he is shot, he must stand up and identify himself.
• Once killed, the Infiltrator then goes back to a designated area. A judge is to be stationed in this area. The Infiltrator is kept there for five minutes and then allowed to re-enter the game.
• If an Infiltrator believes that the Defender does not know exactly where he is, he may wait silently until a judge comes to determine whether the Defender's beam is on him.
• The Infiltrator can be killed inside or outside the perimeter.

Judges: This game requires two judges. One judge is located outside the perimeter in the Infiltrators' cemetery. His job is to time the period the Infiltrators are out of the game. He keeps them there for five minutes.

The other judge is located inside the perimeter. His responsibility is to check out any disputed kills. He does this by going to the spot where the Defender's flashlight beam is located. He declares the Infiltrator dead if he is within the beam. He also declares any Defender out of ammo who uses his flashlight as a searchlight (either as a steady beam or a rapid series of short bursts). It is best to give the Defender a warning before declaring him out of ammo. The Defender is out of ammo for five minutes, then is allowed to resume play.

Winning the game: At the beginning a time limit is set. The Infiltrators win if they capture the flag before the time expires. The Defenders win if they protect their flag the entire time. *Bill Flanders*

JAILBREAK

Have a large group, a large building with several entrances, and a dark night? Then you're set for Jailbreak!

The object is to break into the building, read a message that clues you in to the whereabouts of the treasure, find the treasure, and deliver it to a predetermined leader—all without being caught by guards and imprisoned.

First, divide any number of young people into two teams. Then choose guards: They must be adult leaders or unbiased kids, for the guards must be absolutely neutral, arresting members of both teams impartially. They will patrol the building in pairs, clockwise—never counterclockwise in order to catch players—arresting anyone they can shine their flashlights directly on. When this happens, the guard shouts, "Stop for identification!" The player must stop in his tracks and allow himself to be escorted to jail, where he must remain for 10 minutes or until another player breaks him out.

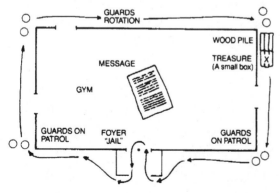

A jailbreak is achieved when a player enters the jail, tags a prisoner, and both of them flee—all without being detected by guards.

What keeps this game active is this: A player earns 100 points for breaking anyone out of jail—even members of the opposing team. Like the guards, the jailer must be an impartial player who never alerts guards, but merely verifies that jailbreaks are legitimate, tallies points for both teams, and settles any disputes.

For more suspense, place a searchlight on the flat roof of the building, and rotate it slowly or turn it on for a few seconds every five minutes or so.

What Jailbreak requires is trust and common honesty. When a patrolman gets you in his beam, for example, the player needs to freeze for the game to continue enjoyably. Prisoners must cooperate as they are escorted to jail. Games with trust factors teach kids the benefits of honesty and fair play—and are great discussion starters for later, too. *Steve Smoker*

MISSION IMPOSSIBLE

This game requires a large field, campgrounds, or woods. The object is for members of two teams to find their team's secret "M" bomb (watermelon) that was stolen and hidden by enemy agents (sponsors). In the process, players shoot each other with squirt guns filled with disappearing ink.

Scattered evenly throughout the playing area are six DMZs. Each of these demilitarized zones are about 25 feet in diameter (marked with flour or lime) and serve as infirmaries and ammunition depots. They're each equipped with a staff person, a pail of disappearing ink (read instructions and dilute properly), and—at the beginning of the game—a third of a team's squirt guns.

Players should wear light-colored shirts in order for the disappearing ink to be seen; teams should be visually distinguishable—different colored squirt guns, armbands, etc.

The game begins this way: While students are gathered at HQ (a meeting hall or other central place) to receive their instructions, a staff member hides the two watermelons in the playing area.

Rules the kids need to hear include these:
• The purpose is to find their team bomb and return it to HQ.
• When players are shot on their shirts, they are considered wounded and must go to the nearest DMZ and wait for the ink to disappear. The

attendant staff member then permits recovered players to rejoin the battle

• While players are refilling their guns in the DMZs, they cannot be shot.

• Recovering players in the DMZ cannot refill their guns, but must wait until they are released and can go to another DMZ to refill.

• If a player finds the bomb but is shot as he's carrying it back to HQ, he must set it down gently (broken melons lose the game for the team that breaks them) and go to the DMZ as usual. Then either a teammate may pick up the bomb and attempt to finish the mission, or an opponent may take the bomb to hide it again.

After these rules are explained to the players, each team has five minutes to discuss their strategy. You may also want to have the initial squirt-gun filling done ahead of time by staff or by a few team members sent to the DMZs while the teams are laying battle plans. You'll probably need a whistle or bell to begin the game and then end it—perhaps after 30 minutes of playing if neither team has won by then.

Afterward, enjoy the watermelons!

Vaughn VanSkiver and Steve Robertson

SMUGGLER

This is a great camp game that is relatively complicated and requires the use of the entire camp area (several acres or so). There are two teams (any number on a team), two territories (divide the camp in half), and each team should be appropriately marked (colored armbands, etc.).

The idea of the game is to smuggle certain items into the other team's territory successfully (without being captured) and make a drop. Points are awarded for successful drops and for capturing smugglers.

The playing area should look something like this:

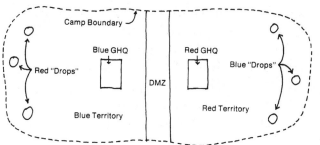

Teams should have names or be designated by color. Each team selects up to 25 percent of its players to be smugglers. They are so identified with an S marked on the back of their hands with a felt-tipped pen. They are the only ones who are allowed to smuggle items into the other team's territory. The rest of the team may capture smugglers from the other team. Smugglers may not capture anyone. Each team should also have a general who is in charge, coordinates team strategy, and remains at all times in the GHQ (General's headquarters).

Camp staff and counselors are neutral and are called U.N. observers. They are positioned on the two teams' territories to maintain order, offer advice, and make sure everyone is playing by the rules of the game. One U.N. observer on each side should be assigned the task of keeping score for that side.

One interesting twist to this game is that each team is allowed a certain number of infiltrators or spies who wear the armbands of one team, but are actually working for the other team. They can be chosen by the game officials prior to the game and secretly informed of their mission. Infiltrators are secretly marked with an X on one leg (or some other place that is relatively hidden). If a player is accused of being an infiltrator, he must show his leg, and tell the truth. If the accusation is correct, the accusing team gets 5,000 points and the infiltrator is taken into custody. He must remain in the GHQ for 10 minutes and is then released to the team he is working for. He gets a new armband and is back in the game, only not as an infiltrator. An incorrect accusation costs the accusing team 5,000 points (points lost). Only the general of each team may make an accusation. If a player suspects a teammate to be a spy, the general is informed and he decides whether or not to accuse. Then the accusation must be made in the presence of a U.N. observer.

The drops are location under rocks, in trees, etc. where a smuggled item may be placed and declared successfully smuggled. Only the smuggling team knows where all the drops are in the opposing team's territory. In other words, the blue team does not know where the red team is attempting to drop items, and vice versa. However, before the game begins, each team locates their drop positions in the other team's territory, and a game official (neutral person) informs the opposing team's general as to the location of half of them. So, the blue team, for example, might know where half of the red team's drops are, and the red team isn't sure which ones they know about. There should be at least four drops for each side. U.N. observers should know where all the drop locations are.

The DMZ is a neutral area that is marked off between the two territories. Anyone may be there without being captured. This is good for strategy, but may be optional.

The game should be played at night. No flashlights are allowed. Because the entire camp is used, buildings, trees, and other obstacles may be used for cover. Unsafe areas should be declared off limits. Players caught in an off-limits area should be penalized by subtracting 5,000 points off their team's score.

The items to be smuggled are simply 3x5 cards with the name of the item on it and its value.

Different items are worth more than others. Points should range anywhere from 1,000 points to 10,000 points. There should be more items of lower point value with the high scoring items being more rare. Any number of items may be used in the game, as long as each team has the same number with the same values. The team's items should be written in ink that matches its color.

As the game progresses, smugglers attempt to get items behind enemy lines and successfully drop them at one of the drop locations in enemy territory. Only one item may be smuggled at one time by a smuggler. Once a drop is made (successfully), the smuggler raises his hand and yells "U. N." until he finds or is found by a U. N. observer. The U. N. observer then verifies the drop and escorts him back to his own territory where points are awarded. While a smuggler has his hand raised and is yelling "U.N.," he may not be captured by the enemy. Faking this procedure is a rule infraction that costs 5,000 points.

If the smuggler is captured during his smuggling attempt, he is brought to the GHQ of the capturing team and must remain there for 10 minutes before being released. (This time can vary.) He also gets a mark on his hand in the capturing team's color. The mark keeps the capturing team up-to-date on how many times he has been caught. Every time a smuggler is captured, the appropriate score is tallied, and the smuggled item is confiscated.

In the face of imminent capture, a smuggler may dump the item he is attempting to smuggle and hope that it will not be discovered or that it might be picked up by a fellow smuggler. If the capturing team finds it, they may turn it in for its face value.

Smugglers may be captured any number of ways, depending on how rough or messy you want to get. They may be tagged, tackled, hit with a water balloon, or perhaps hit with a nylon stocking full of flour. Choose your own method.

Scoring:
• A successful drop is worth 1,000 points plus the value of the item.
• An extra 2,000 points is earned if the smuggler can make a successful drop and return to his own team's territory without being captured by the enemy or escorted back by a U.N. observer.
• On capturing a smuggler, the capturing team gets points in the following manner.

First time caught: 500 points plus half the value of the item being smuggled.

Second time caught: 1,500 points plus full value of item.

Third time caught: 3,000 points plus full value of item.
• Correctly identifying an infiltrator is worth 5,000 points. Incorrectly accusing one costs 5,000 points.
• Any item found bearing the opposing team's color may be turned in for the full value of the item.

Keith Geckeler

SPACE WAR

Here is a wide game that works best with teams of 50 to 75 each. Be sure you use good balloons that do not break easy.

There are two teams: the Rebels (orange balloons) and the Galactic Empire (green balloons). The Rebels are led by Luke Skywaddler and are divided into small groups each commanded by a Sky Colonel. The Galactic Forces are commanded by the dreaded Derth Vector and are likewise divided into small groups each led by a Space Commander. The battlefield consists of a very large area that is divided into two spaces. In the Rebel Space there will be five clearly identified and well-spaced-out air bases and one P.O.W. area. From these five air bases, the Rebels will launch their attack. In the Galactic

Empire Space there are five clearly identified and well-spaced-out life control recepticals (L.C.R.'s) and one P.O.W. camp. The L.C.R.'s can be ordinary garbage cans. Each player should have a green or orange balloon attached (tied) to his or her wrist. These are known as life support tanks.

The object of the game is to destroy the enemy by "de-lifing" enemy soldiers, destroying air bases, bombing L.C.R.'s., de-lifing either Derth Vector or Luke Skywaddler and thus making as many points as possible in the 45 minutes of play. The rules and instructions below should be given to each player.

Points are awarded as follows:
• 100 points for each enemy soldier de-lifed and carried to your team's P.O.W. area.
• 500 points for each air base or life control receptical destroyed.
• 1,000 points for de-lifing and carrying to your team's P.O.W. area either Derth Vector or Luke Skywaddler.

Team with the most points after penalties wins!

General rules of play:
• All combat is by hand only. You de-life an opponent by popping her balloon. No tripping, shoving, tackling, strangling, or holding allowed. The second the balloon is popped the player is de-lifed.
• Once are de-lifed, that's it. The player is dead weight until the end of the game.
• To get points for de-lifed enemy soldiers, they must be carried or dragged to the P.O.W. area. Guys can only drag or carry guys. Girls can only drag or carry girls.
• Rebel bombs destroy life control recepticals by either dropping or throwing a bomb into this container before being de-lifed. A game judge at the site will be judge of this. No attempt can be made to move or displace life control recepticals. No attempt can be made to block or bat away a bomb once it is thrown. The only defense allowed is to de-life bombs. Once the L.C.R. has been successfully bombed, it is turned upside down. Bombs can be yellow balloons—one given to each Rebel.
• The Galactic forces destroy Rebel air bases by gaining control of the official air base sign and tearing it in half before being de-lifed. This sign can in no way be held or touched by Rebel forces.

• Neither team can employ the defense or offense of a "human ring" or wall around or against an air base or L.C.R. by joining hands or locking arms. Each player must be a free agent at all times.
• Derth Vector and Luke Skywaddler have two balloons, one on each wrist. Both of these must be destroyed if either of these are to be immobilized.
• All buildings are off limits.
• If your balloon accidentally pops—too bad!

Penalties:
• 100 points per incident of failing to fall dead immediately after having one's balloon popped.
• 300 points per incident for unnecessary roughness.
• 300 points per incident for failure to obey a game judge immediately. Judges will be watching all activity. It will do no good to accuse or complain about enemy activity.

Good luck and may the force be with you!

Phil Kennemer

SPY GAME

This game only takes about an hour to play, but the planning and the excitement can take several days.

Early in the week the camp director selects certain kids to be the spies. The only ones who know the identities of the spies are the camp director and the head spy who is also chosen by the camp director. Each spy is given a spy badge (a small card) which they can hide or conceal on their persons. During the actual game they must carry the card with them. During the week leading up to the game, there can be a lot of rumors spread about who the spies are. This is one fun aspect of the game.

There should be no more than 25 spies, or about one-fourth of the camp, whichever is smaller. Everyone else is a cop, although even the spies pretend to be cops. Sometime during the week the head spy can call some secret meetings of the spies to discuss strategy and to make sure that everyone is doing a good job of keeping their identity as a spy a secret.

The objective of the spies is to drop a bomb into a designated area of the camp. If this game is played at a week-long camp (Sunday through Friday), then the game could be scheduled for Friday, say from 11:00 a.m. to noon (one hour). It is during this time that the spies try to make the drop.

The bomb can be anything you want. For example, it could be an old briefcase stuffed with secret documents. The bomb should be kept on display all week. The designated area where the drop must be made could be a garbage can, the back of a certain pickup truck, or something similar.

When the game actually starts, the spies are given the bomb, and it is the cops' duty to prevent the bomb from getting into the designated area.

They can kill spies by taking away their secret spy badges. A person who is suspected of being a spy is taken to the camp director (or other official), who may take the person's spy badge, and the spy is out of the game. No cops may be within 500 feet of the designated area where the bomb is to be dropped, unless they see the bomb inside that area. If the bomb is successfully dropped, then the spies win and the game is over. If the bomb is captured by the cops, or if all the spies are killed, then the cops win and the game is over.

This game is most effective if much planning has been done in advance. The spies should figure out a good way to pose as cops while secretly hiding the bomb and getting it delivered at just the right time to the designated bomb-dropping area. The cops should be trying to figure out all week who the spies are, so that when the game starts, they can begin rounding them up. *Jerry Cramer*

VELCRO WAR

For this textile tag game, go to a craft store and purchase golf-ball-size plastic balls and Velcro strips. Use a hot-glue gun to attach the strips to the balls. (The more balls you have, the better the game.)

Then declare a Velcro war among the kids. All combatants must wear a fluffy wool sweater to qualify them to carry weapons (the prepared plastic balls). They should also wear some kind of eye protection. In the church or at a school, identify a playing area that includes lots of hiding places accessible by more than one route.

The following rules will get you started. Once it's all-out war, make up the rules as you go along.
• Once a Velcro ball sticks, it's a wound. It can't be taken off. Three wounds equal a kill.
• Play the game as teams. The smaller the group, however, the better it is to play every man for himself.

• You may expand the target area by requiring all players to wear wool caps.
• The harder the throw, the less likely balls are to stick and the more likely they are to injure, so attack with lobs and crafty tosses.
Dik LaPine

WAR

Any number of kids can play. The entire crowd is divided up into two armies, the Red Army and the Black Army. (You can come up with more creative names for the armies if you prefer.) Each army has a general and is identified by red or black armbands, which cannot be removed during the game.

The object of the game is to destroy the opponent's radar installation. This is done by dropping a bomb on it.

Each army should have its own territory. Half the playing area should be assigned to each army and marked appropriately.

Both armies are divided up into two units: the offensive and the defensive. The offensive unit's mission is to seek and destroy the opponent's radar installation, and is under the command of a colonel. The offensive unit is also divided into platoons of from five to seven members each. Each platoon has a captain and a lieutenant (who is second in command). The offensive unit has no boundary restrictions. These players may go anywhere to accomplish their mission.

The defensive unit of each army has the same organization as the offensive unit (with the same leadership and platoons), but the mission is to protect its own radar station and to repel the invading offensive unit of the opposing army. This unit may not enter the territory of the other army.

The radar installations are two containers (preferably brightly colored) placed on the ground somewhere in each of the two armies' territories. They cannot be camouflaged or hidden. They must be easily visible to the opposing army once the opposing army gets near to it.

Each army gets a certain number of bombs (25 or so). A live bomb is a plastic bottle (or any small container) containing a jelly bean that is the color of the respective army. A deactivated bomb is a plastic bottle without a jelly bean. Only the offensive units of each army are allowed to carry bombs. In order to destroy the opponent's radar installation, a live bomb must be dropped into it. The defensive soldiers may seize bombs from their opponents and deactivate them by destroying the jelly bean (eating it). The captured bomb may then be activated by the capturing team with a new jelly bean of its own color, making its own army a little stronger. (The more bombs an army has, the better chance it has of getting one in to the opposing army's radar station successfully.)

Other weapons are used in the game as well. Guns are felt-tipped pens. Generals and colonels have two each. Each captain has one for his platoon. No other players may carry guns. Guns may also be captured from opposing players.

To shoot an opponent, he must first be captured. Capturing a player is done simply by grabbing him and holding him down (overpowering him). A captured player is then shot by having one finger of the left hand marked with a felt-tipped pen (gun). The opponent is then released. He cannot be pursued for two minutes, or recaptured by anyone for two minutes. Also he may not attack the radar station or one of his opponents for the same length of time. A player is dead and out of the game when he has had four fingers on his left hand marked (shot four times). He then must report to the camp and remain there until the game is over. (If you prefer, you may recycle dead players by allowing them to wait 10 minutes, then marking a big purple heart or some other identification on the palm of their left hand, and then returning to the game. They can then be shot four more times on their right hand.)

The game is over when either radar has been bombed three times with a live bomb. At that point a signal will be sounded and all the players must return to the center of the camp. The losing general and his colonels may then be executed by getting a pie in the face.

This game can be changed or adapted as you see fit. It can be played with more than two armies as well. Playing time is usually about an hour or so, including time for each army to get organized. *Jerry Summers*

This is a fun game for groups of over 50 kids. It is excellent for camps and can be followed up the next day with a total disarmament game or cease-fire game which involves feeding the hungry, clothing the naked, or whatever. The purpose of this game is simply to win the war. This is done by destroying the enemy and capturing or killing their general.

Necessary props:
• Water balloons. These are used as bombs, mortar shells, hand grenades, etc.
• Armbands of various colors to identify everyone. For example, have a red army versus a blue army, by using appropriate colored bands on the right arm. Also another color of armband can be used on the left arm to signify whether the person is air force, artillery, etc.
• Plenty of room to do battle with good hiding places.
• Nonmilitary supervisors to make sure all the rules of the game are being followed. These people have the power to kill or heal at will. They should be equipped with whistles to start and stop the game, call violations, etc.
• An area marked off for the military graveyard.

Personnel involved and their roles:
• **General:** Each army has a commander-in-chief. The general wears either a red or blue armband, plus a bright yellow band worn across the chest (Miss America style). The generals may only be killed by having their armbands or generals' bands ripped off—they can't be killed by mortars, bombs, grenades, etc. (The idea here is that the generals are usually well protected in bunkers, and not susceptible to artillery attack or strafing. They must be killed or captured only in hand-to-hand combat.)
• **Air Force:** These are the only people in the game allowed to run. Everybody else walks. (The nonmilitary supervisors carefully enforce this. Violators must remove their armbands and retire to the military graveyard.) Air force people wear their army bands on their right arms and light blue bands on their left arms. They may only carry two water balloons at a time. (Any air force person with more than two bombs is supposed to have crashed due to overloading and must head to the graveyard after removing their armband.) Air force players may run

in and out of any situation with two bombs. They may strafe any person except generals. (Anyone with water on them is considered dead.) Air force may also run up to any person, take off either armband, and run away. If the armband which represents artillery, air force, etc., is taken, but the armband signifying either red or blue army remains, that person becomes infantry. (In order to capture a general, air force personnel may run into the general's bunker, tear off the air force insignia from her own arm, thus becoming a paratrooper. Once the air force insignia is off, however, the person may only walk and may carry no bombs.)

• **Artillery:** These soldiers may only walk and are signified by a green armband on the left arm and a red or blue band on the right arm. They are allowed as many water balloons as they can carry and may attack anyone with them. They can also function as refilling (re-arming) stations for the air force. Once their artillery insignia is torn off, however, they may no longer touch water balloons, even to hide or destroy them.

• **Infantry:** These are the backbone of the armies. They only wear a red or blue band. They may only walk, but can kill anyone they come across. They should be used to protect the artillery and the generals.

Further instructions:
• Bombs and cannon shells (water balloons) are lethal to anyone who gets wet from them, including the thrower.

• Infantry may destroy the enemy supply of balloons by poking them with a stick. They may not, however, pick them up for any reason.

• Game ends when one general is either killed or captured.

• You can make the game interesting by setting sprinklers going here and there as mine fields. You can also rope off strategic paths as radioactive. Anyone entering a radioactive area is dead and sent to the graveyard.

• Once dead, the person cannot kill anyone and may not divulge any information.

John Splinter

YOUTH SPECIALTIES TITLES

Professional Resources

Administration, Publicity, & Fundraising (Ideas Library)

Developing Student Leaders

Equipped to Serve: Volunteer Youth Worker Training Course

Help! I'm a Junior High Youth Worker!

Help! I'm a Sunday School Teacher!

Help! I'm a Volunteer Youth Worker!

How to Expand Your Youth Ministry

How to Speak to Youth...and Keep Them Awake at the Same Time

One Kid at a Time: Reaching Youth through Mentoring

A Youth Ministry Crash Course

The Youth Worker's Handbook to Family Ministry

Youth Ministry Programming

Camps, Retreats, Missions, & Service Ideas (Ideas Library)

Compassionate Kids: Practical Ways to Involve Your Students in Mission and Service

Creative Bible Lessons in John: Encounters with Jesus

Creative Bible Lessons in Romans: Faith on Fire!

Creative Bible Lessons on the Life of Christ

Creative Junior High Programs from A to Z, Vol. 1 (A-M)

Creative Meetings, Bible Lessons, & Worship Ideas (Ideas Library)

Crowd Breakers & Mixers (Ideas Library)

Drama, Skits, & Sketches (Ideas Library)

Dramatic Pauses

Facing Your Future: Graduating Youth Group with a Faith That Lasts

Games (Ideas Library)

Games 2 (Ideas Library)

Great Fundraising Ideas for Youth Groups

Great Retreats for Youth Groups

Greatest Skits on Earth

Greatest Skits on Earth, Vol. 2

Holiday Ideas (Ideas Library)

Hot Illustrations for Youth Talks

Incredible Questionnaires for Youth Ministry

Junior High Game Nights

Kickstarters: 101 Ingenious Intros to Just about Any Bible Lesson

Memory Makers

More Great Fundraising Ideas for Youth Groups

More Hot Illustrations for Youth Talks

More Junior High Game Nights

Play It Again! More Great Games for Groups

Play It! Great Games for Groups

Special Events (Ideas Library)

Spontaneous Melodramas

Super Sketches for Youth Ministry

Teaching the Bible Creatively

Up Close and Personal: How to Build Community in Your Youth Group

Wild Truth Bible Lessons

Worship Services for Youth Groups

Discussion Starter Resources

Discussion & Lesson Starters (Ideas Library)

Discussion & Lesson Starters 2 (Ideas Library)

4th-6th Grade TalkSheets

Get 'Em Talking

High School TalkSheets

High School TalkSheets: Psalms and Proverbs

Junior High TalkSheets

Junior High TalkSheets: Psalms and Proverbs

Keep 'Em Talking!

More High School TalkSheets

More Junior High TalkSheets

Parent Ministry TalkSheets

What If...? 450 Thought-Provoking Questions to Get Teenagers Talking, Laughing, and Thinking

Would You Rather...? 465 Provocative Questions to Get Teenagers Talking

Clip Art

ArtSource Vol. 1—Fantastic Activities

ArtSource Vol. 2—Borders, Symbols, Holidays, and Attention Getters

ArtSource Vol. 3—Sports

ArtSource Vol. 4—Phrases and Verses

ArtSource Vol. 5—Amazing Oddities and Appalling Images

ArtSource Vol. 6—Spiritual Topics

ArtSource Vol. 7—Variety Pack

ArtSource Vol. 8CStark Raving Clip Art

ArtSource CD-ROM (contains Vols. 1-7)

Videos

Edge TV

The Heart of Youth Ministry: A Morning with Mike Yaconelli

Next Time I Fall in Love Video Curriculum

Understanding Your Teenager Video Curriculum

Student Books

Grow For It Journal

Grow For It Journal through the Scriptures

Wild Truth Journal for Junior Highers